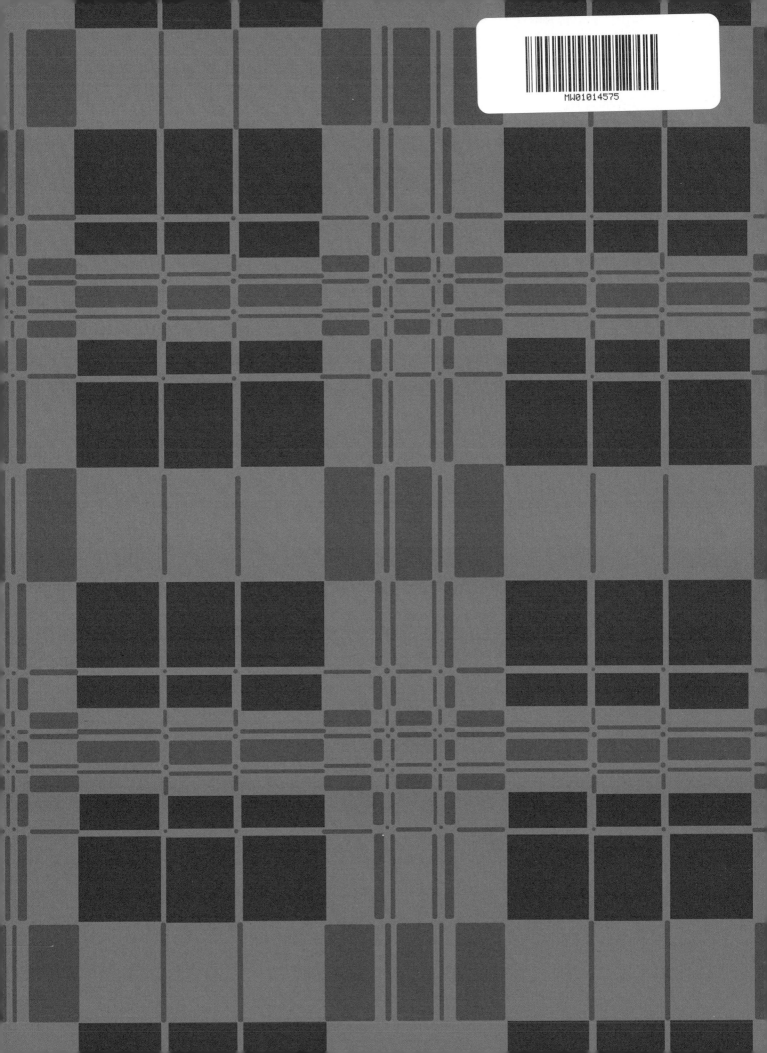

MW01014575

Design Commune

Roman Alonso and Steven Johanknecht
with a foreword by Matt Tyrnauer
and in conversation with Mayer Rus

Abrams, New York

FOREWORD: The Southland

When it comes to making observations and depictions of Los Angeles, outsiders almost always have a more interesting perspective and a greater ability to interpret and synthesize the mercurial culture of the city. Of course, the rare native occasionally hits the bullseye. Bret Easton Ellis, for example, who singlehandedly defined certain aspects of the 1980s for the permanent record; likewise, Walter Mosley and James Ellroy for the 1930s and 1940s; and Robert Towne for the late 1930s and the 1970s, and P.T. Anderson for the 1990s. And yet, consider just some of the visitors and transplants who have been the main cultural interpreters, and, ultimately, the most heroic definers of the place: David Hockney (West Yorkshire, UK); James M. Cain (Annapolis, Maryland); Ed Ruscha (Omaha, Nebraska); Evelyn Waugh (London, UK); F. Scott Fitzgerald (St. Paul, Minnesota); Jessica Mitford (Gloucestershire, UK); Hal Ashby (Ogden, Utah); Charles and Henry Greene (Brighton, Ohio); Joan Didion (Sacramento, California).

Los Angeles, as a city of immigrants, self-selectors, and self-reinventors, is a place where, as the historian Garry Wills once observed, the "natives arrived the day before yesterday rather than yesterday." Thus, the Southland, as the greater city is disconcertingly called by local newscasters, has been, since mid-century, the ultimate American arrival city, willing and able to absorb and nurture a diverse array of cultures, many of whom have been pleased to discover a zone of creative free expression, far less hemmed in than eastern cities—particularly New York—by societal strictures and the rules of the game. LA is a giant, commodious, at times puzzling but liberating blank slate. This essential characteristic has allowed many creative minds to work at full tilt and dispense with a lot of the dues-paying that other more hidebound cities require.

No other field has benefited more from the city's liberal attitude toward artistic endeavor than architecture and design. In a town where there was no historic tradition to which to adhere (the once-prevalent "Spanish" theme of LA architecture is just that, a theme, riffing off of the Pueblo Revival style of the Spanish colonists, itself a riff on colonial architecture south of the border) the tabula rasa proved a blessing. By the 1920s, Rudolph Schindler and Richard Neutra, both from Vienna and both one-time associates of Frank Lloyd Wright (from Richland Center, Wisconsin), were working in Los Angeles in competition with Wright, and redefining Modernism in America with their houses, apartments, and mixed-use structures all over the region. They, in turn, had been influenced by the radical early California modernist Irving Gill (originally from Tully, New York). The 1922 Schindler House, at 833 Kings Road in West Hollywood, was a watershed moment for Modernism, considered to be one of the most important houses of its time, both for its avant-garde precast "lift slab" concrete construction, and for its function as a communal live-work compound. Schindler and his wife, Pauline, in fact, shared the house with Neutra and his wife, Dione, for five years in the 1920s, setting a provocative and resonant precedent for a kind of Bohemianism in what was then not-quite-yet the movie capital of the world, but a provincial, emerging city set among orange groves, barley, and oil fields between the Santa Monica Mountains and the Pacific coast. Once again, outsiders were pushing things forward in lotusland. Who would have guessed that Viennese Modernism would adapt well on the Pacific Rim?

In the late 1970s, as a child, I saw the Schindler House for the first time. My parents brought me to a party there being thrown by a group of hippies, who had adopted it for their urban commune, at a time when the general population of LA didn't give a damn about Schindler or Neutra's Modernism, and many aging Modern houses were considered to be eyesores and labeled "tear-downs." As squalid as the house was, stripped of most of its original fixtures (Schindler died in 1953), I remember being beguiled. It all seemed very edgy, different, and even dangerous (though that may have had something to do with the exposed, frayed wiring hanging out everywhere, and the cracked linoleum laid over the original cement floors). It was my first true awareness of LA Modernism and it suddenly reoriented me and inspired me to seek out the neglected and hidden Modern architectural history of my hometown.

In a book cataloguing the best of LA architecture by Charles Moore, then dean of the architecture department at UCLA, I found the rest of Schindler and Neutra's buildings. My friends and I diligently went to see them all, knocking on the doors of the houses, asking for tours. Frequently, the people who had commissioned the houses were still living in them. They were delighted to have a gang of middle-school students interested in their homes. The most important house closest to where I lived was the Eames House (built, in 1949, as part of the Case Study House Program sponsored by *Arts & Architecture Magazine*), which sits on a bluff overlooking the Pacific, near Santa Monica. My friends and I, with trepidation, used to gun our cars up the steep driveway, and then get out and walk about the Eames property. We'd linger in the famous meadow in front of the iconic structure, and peer into the windows of the living room, where all of Charles and Ray Eames's craft objects were on display, just where Ray, who was still living in the house at the time, had placed them. Ray never appeared. Charles had died more than a decade before.

How powerful it was to see that Eames living room intact! The taxonomic array of the Eames' craft and textile and furniture collections in the living room contrasting wholly with the clean, minimalist lines of the glass-and-steel house. It was a study in bold contradiction and enormous aesthetic confidence, and it had, at one time, been the nerve center and creative incubator of the vastly influential Eames operation, which was, much like the Schindler House of its day, a design commune.

The Eameses (he, originally from St. Louis, and she, a native of Sacramento), met at the Cranbrook Academy of Art in Bloom-field Hills, Michigan. They set out in 1941 on a "honeymoon road trip," which led the couple to relocate permanently to Los Angeles. Their first residence, after putting up in a hotel for a time, was Neutra's Strathmore Apartments in Westwood. Charles and Ray began molding their famous plywood into chairs in the second bedroom of the apartment. They soon found more adequate work spaces on Abbott Kinney Boulevard in Venice, which became the storied Eames Office, the most significant multi-disciplinary design studio in the United States, if not the world—and a next-generation version of the collective/collaborative notions of Schindler and Neutra a generation before. The Eames Office produced an astonishing array of architecture, industrial design products, textiles, and even a string of award-winning films, all infused with an optimistic and accessible design approach that did much to define mid-century modern American life. The Eames Office's holistic approach to design across disciplines was its hallmark, and, thanks in large part to the dynamic partnership of Charles and Ray, as well as the charismatic master salesmanship of Charles, the Eames Office became the ne plus ultra of industrial design in LA (and far beyond), with hooks into every commercial sphere of consequence: aerospace, military, government, architecture, and consumer product design, both for the carriage trade as well as the mass market. The success—as well as the publicity—was enormous and lasting. Moreover, they made it look so *easy*. Of course, none of it was easy. The Eameses—and the design team that supported them—were, in fact, outliers, whose acumen and celebrity inoculated them against the potentially deadly forces of suspicion that ruled life in mid-century America. It wasn't all groovy optimism: It was also the McCarthy era, when anything collective or communal—or obviously foreign as Schindler and Neutra were—was considered suspicious. The special Southern California subsect of McCarthyite politics, the John Birch Society, was particularly alert to any artistic type who could be pegged or smeared as a pinko or a degenerate, or both. If the more radical (and less successful) Schindler had lived past 1953, he may have been ostracized totally. Thus, as a measure of self-preservation, the Eames Office and Richard Neutra were loaded up with patriotic government contracts, which not only paid the bills, but mitigated any suspicions of radical un-American activities in their respective studios. They survived and thrived, and coaxed the ethos and the cityscape of the Southland.

Neutra died in 1970, and Charles Eames died in 1978, and, sadly, the era of integral California Modern they did much to create, virtually died along with them. The High Modern architecture heritage of the city was almost entirely neglected in the last decades of the 20th century, treated like a cute fad, misunderstood, abandoned, and frequently slated for obliteration. As real estate values drive almost every aspect of life in Southern California, the Modernism of the city was doomed by realtors and developers, who brought on an era of faux Baroque McMansions and strip malls in the style of gigantic Taco Bells or a seven-car garage designed by Michael Graves. The aesthetics of Orange County—seat of the John Birch Society—were encroaching on, and nearly overtaking, the more human-scaled, individualistic domestic architecture of the County of Angels. When would, or could, the madness stop?

There were, in the years before the turn of the millennium, some signs of hope, among them the revival of interest in the unloved Modern houses, which became known as mid-century Modern houses. Architecture groupies began to buy and restore them. Preservation movements took hold, and a new generation of designers began to refer to the LA Modern aesthetic in their work, and, more vitally, these designers could find work from tastemakers and thought leaders who were obsessively restoring the iconic, surviving examples of domestic Modern architecture. The structures gained totemic status. They were no longer mere houses; they were sculptures to collect—and to live in.

As a correspondent for *Vanity Fair* magazine at that time, part of my job was to record and canonize these acts of architectural mercy. One day, Helmut Newton alerted me that a friend of his, the German publisher, Benedikt Taschen, was restoring John Lautner's 1960 Chemosphere house, which looms over Mulholland Drive like a wood-and-glass flying saucer.

Helmut and I went over to see Taschen, and he did a spontaneous photo shoot in the Chemosphere. As Helmut had neglected to bring a tripod, he asked his photo assistant to lock him in a bear hug to make the shot stable. Helmut clicked away, bellowing the whole time, "Hold me, baby! Hold me, baby!"

I wrote the story of the house and Taschen's fascination with Los Angeles for the magazine. Taschen, a major art collector, who runs a salon out of the Chemosphere living room, soon befriended his next-door neighbor, David Hockney. Now Hockney is a regular on the built-in banquettes in a conversation nook of the Chemosphere living room. Each time I witness the ex-patriot publisher from Cologne, Germany, and the son of Yorkshire —collector and maestro—together in conversation next to Lautner's mod hearth at the center of the lovingly restored spaceship house, I feel as if I am observing a baton being passed between the outsider/emigres who continue to define high culture of the city. Through the CinemaScope picture windows of Lautner's masterpiece, the light grid of the city that beguiles us all spreads out toward the silhouetted mountain backdrop.

Around the same time I wrote this story about Taschen and the Chemosphere, I was asked to write another article about a new design firm that was taking off in town. It seemed to me that Commune, founded in 2004, was at once a throwback and a harbinger. As the name announces, the firm takes a collectivist approach to its work—shades of the Eameses—and its two lead designers, Roman Alonso and Steven Johanknecht, have a deep knowledge and abiding appreciation of the design heritage of the city they work in. At the time, in 2007, they had just created a store on Rodeo Drive that was a throwback to the luxurious brutalism of the '60s and '70s era of travertine temples for Gucci and Neiman Marcus. It was a welcome break from the faux Via Condotti wave that overtook Beverly Hills shopping streets in the 1990s—yet another symptom of Orange County's imagineered sensibilities overtaking LA.

Sixteen years on from the *Vanity Fair* piece, it's clear that Commune was, in fact, the leading edge of what has become an arts and design revolution in Los Angeles, fueled by creative people across many disciplines, flocking to the city, where rents for studio spaces are still comparatively reasonable—certainly in relation to New York and London. Commune itself has also stoked the flames of this LA arts Renaissance by commissioning an astonishing roster of artists, craftspeople, and artisans (many based in the city) to collaborate with them on their projects. The long list includes Alma Allen (sculpture and furniture); Lisa Eisner (bibelot and objet); Stan Bitters (ceramic sculpture); Adam Silverman (ceramics); Tanya Aguiñiga (fiber art); the Haas Brothers (mixed media and murals); Adam Pogue (textiles); Samiro Yunoki (textiles and illustration); Ido Yoshimoto (wood sculpture and furniture); Louis Eisner (murals).

In the *Vanity Fair* article, Johanknecht told me, "We are facilitators not dictators," pointing to a more idealistic form of communism—if you will—which harkens back to the shared studio/home of Schindler, and the creative impulses that made the "city of future" idealism of LA so attractive to the pre-war generation of designers who migrated here from Europe, the eastern architecture schools, or, like the Eameses, the multi-disciplinary, crafts-oriented Cranbrook Art Academy outside of Detroit.

It goes without saying that Alonso and Johanknecht are both from somewhere else. Alonso was born in Caracas, Venezuela, and later moved to Miami, before starting his career in Manhattan in fashion PR. Johanknecht is from Syracuse, New York, and, before he relocated to Manhattan, commuted to New York City on $20 People's Express weekend flights to attend Studio 54. The pair first worked together at Barneys New York as members of an in-house creative team, responsible for everything from the store interiors to the display windows to advertising, and the famous no-expense-spared launch parties, a hallmark of the era when the Pressman family still presided over what turned out to be the last glorious gasp of the department store era.

Alonso noted in *Vanity Fair* that when clients come to their first meetings with Commune, "We really make them talk to us almost like therapy sessions, and bring totemic objects." The totemic objects in the Eames living room come to mind. These were moved around and rearranged obsessively by Ray Eames, and are as integral to the iconic house as the boxy steel girder construction and the colored panels of the facade. The cool minimalism of the High Modern, cut with the expressive taste of the inhabitants. Alonso and Johanknecht's instincts are, likewise, to make things that are bespoke and personal, and as far from standardized and overly manufactured as possible. "We help clients find their genetic make-up and develop their own language and style," said Johanknecht. According to Alonso, "Steven and I have never been afraid to step outside what's usually expected of a more conventional design studio. Size or type of project or style is not the most important thing. What we love most is an interesting challenge and diversity for the team. Many studios have a signature look, and although some people would say we do, we don't see it that way. We work hard to bring out what should be our client's aesthetic. We help them figure out what their world should look like. If we are successful, it looks right for them." They are, in effect, helping you channel your inner Ray Eames.

The diversity and range of Commune's various projects bears this out: The Ace Hotels, including the Palm Springs and Los Angeles branches, are definitive examples of adaptive reuse—the former touching off a new wave of hotels in the desert that have sensitively reinterpreted Palm Springs Modernism, and the latter reviving an entire swath of LA's early-20th-century downtown theater district. Stores for Heath, the California pottery concern, create a casual sense of artisanal luxe, and likewise, a meticulous Spanish Colonial home restoration in the Los Feliz section of LA. At the other end of the California vernacular design spectrum is Commune's reinterpretation of a craftsman house in Berkeley.

Branching out from their Los Angeles home base, and disseminating the Commune ethos, the group is behind the Goop flagship in Manhattan; the Caldera House ski club in Jackson Hole, Wyoming, and an Ace Hotel in Kyoto. "The design of the Ace Kyoto," says Alonso, "is rooted in the idea of East meets West through craft. Both Japan and California have a long tradition and respect for craft, and the inspiration came from the cultural exchange brought about by Japanese Americans like Isamu Noguchi, Ruth Asawa, and George Nakashima, and from the collaboration between western designers, like Charlotte Perriand, and Japanese craftsmen. For the project, we actually recruited a long list of Japanese artists and artisans, as well as Californians. The only American artists and craftsmen working on the project are from California, so it's kind of Kyoto meets West Coast." Moreover, he adds, "The architect on the project is Kengo Kuma, who has never collaborated with an American interior designer, so in that sense it's also Japan meets California."

The Commune office, with their collaborators and in-house designers, who work in teams, has the air of a laid-back Wiener

Werkstätte. One notes that the computer screens around the office are not only filled with renderings of interiors, but also of textiles, rugs, tiles, super graphics, furniture. They even have a line of chocolate in collaboration with Valerie Gordon, the confectionary queen of the fast-gentrifying LA neighborhood Echo Park. Confectionary queen, bespoke design studio, and Echo Park were not categories that went together just a handful of years ago—yet another example of how Commune has been a catalyst for making LA a cultural loadstar in the present time.

"Four years ago, we got rid of all hierarchy in the studio—teams, departments, etc.," says Johanknecht. "Now we are truly an open studio where our designers work as one large team and are involved in some way on all projects. To us, designing a poster, a napkin, a chair, a trailer, a house, or a hotel is all the same. We see it first and foremost as problem solving." Alonso adds, "Our staff"—which currently numbers twenty—"reflects Steven's and my background and interests. Varied and unexpected. Fine artists, an architect with a masters from Harvard, a doctor in sociology, former industrial designers, etc. They all have a love of the type of work we do and are team players. Those are the only true requirements for entry."

Johanknecht concludes, "We've never been stuck on being anything in particular or been precious about what we do. We've always been honest about who and what we are. We simply see ourselves as a full-service design studio that is always open for collaboration and for business."

I recently asked Alonso and Johanknecht to survey their Commune team to see how many of them are, like the majority of the key designers of the Southland aesthetic, from somewhere else. "Only three are from LA," Alonso says.

Migrants, as ever, shape the land.

Matt Tyrnauer
Los Angeles, January 2020

Page 9: Living room, Berkeley Hills, California, 2017. A Hammerhead chair by Michael Boyd is paired with a vintage rosewood desk. The Josef Hoffmann sconce is by Woka Lamps Vienna.

Previous: Living room, Berkeley Hills, California, 2017. The client wanted a house that was beautiful but completely user friendly; their two young children do their homework and play in this living room. They love Viennese design and Brazilian furniture, which was an influence—and we wanted to honor the craftsman style but also to be unexpected. The sofas are custom and the coffee table is by Alma Allen.

Left: Entry hall and powder room, San Francisco, California, 2019. The walnut entry mirror is made by Tripp Carpenter, who's based in Bolinas, California. In the powder room, the brass and soapstone vanity is designed by Commune, and the mirror was handcrafted by Chris French in San Francisco. The umbrella stand is 1950s Italian.

Above: Dining room, San Francisco, California, 2019. This formal dining room opens into both the kitchen and the inner courtyard. The table is custom-made by Tripp Carpenter. The chairs are by BDDW. The silk and wool rug is our Kaleidoscope pattern for Christopher Farr. The pendant is vintage Vilhelm Lauritzen, and the woven wall hanging is by Kris Dey, ca. 1977.

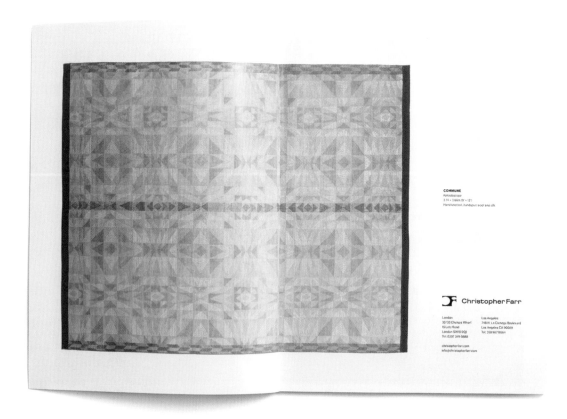

Above: A Christopher Farr ad for our Kaleidoscope rug in *World of Interiors*, 2017.

Right: Foyer, Berkeley Hills, California, 2017. Scarlett reads on an Ole Wanscher daybed by Carl Hansen & Son under a painting by Fred Reichman and sconce by Fernando Santangelo.

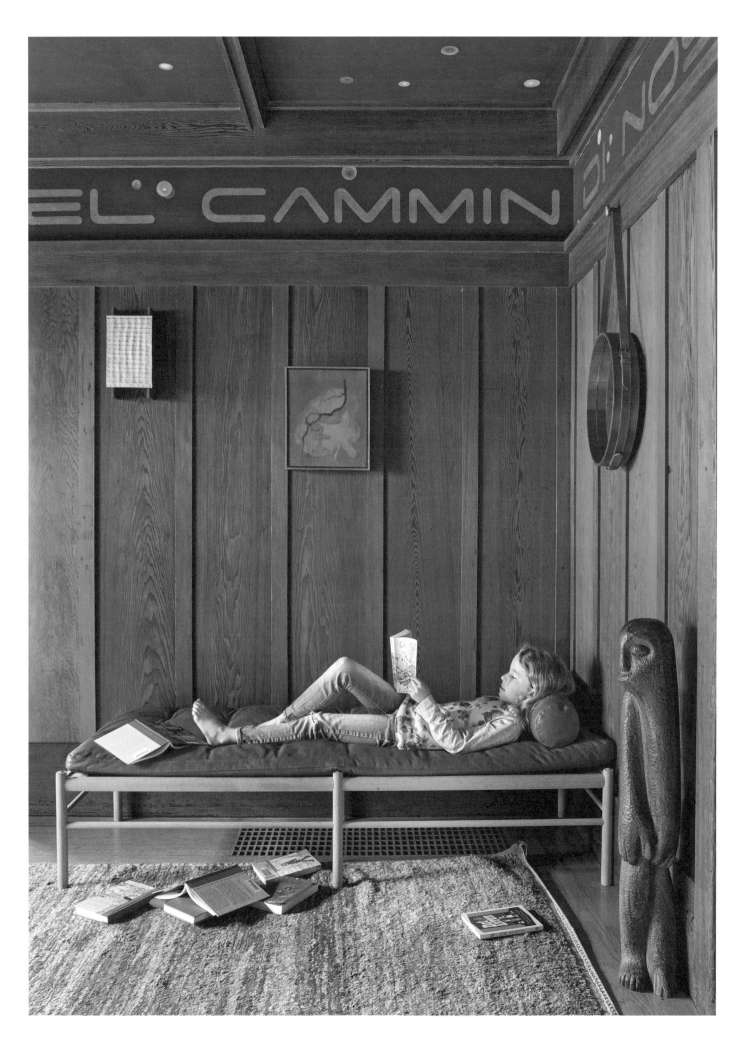

Above: Cast-brass arrowhead door pull, part of Lisa Eisner's Nugget hardware collection for Commune, 2016.

Right: Dining room, Los Angeles, California, 2016.

Left: Dining room, Los Angeles, California, 2016. A Commune custom-designed silk and jute rug and an Art Deco dining table is paired with vintage Brazilian dining chairs. A Paul Evans cabinet is beneath the window, a print by James Welling hangs on the wall, and the centerpiece on the table is an Ettore Sottsass bowl.

Above: Child's room, San Francisco, California, 2019. The children's bedrooms were inspired by ship's cabins. The client liked the idea of rooms just for sleeping with a larger separate playroom attached so the kids would spend as little time as possible in their bedrooms. Like the rest of the house, all wall paneling and millwork is salvaged claro walnut, and the floors and ceiling are locally sourced elm.

Following: Living room, West Marin, California, 2016. The client wanted a refined camping experience for this family compound in Northern California. The rug is a Swedish pattern custom woven in wool and goat hair by Amadi Carpets, and the yellow plaid sofa is Vincent Van Duysen for Gubi. The ottoman is by Axel Vervoordt. The console is Egg Collective. The coffee table base was made in Utah from a hollowed out boulder. The striped sofa is by Tripp Carpenter from a design his father, Arthur Espenet Carpenter, made for the Mill Valley Library. The chairs are vintage Arne Norell, and the paintings are vintage Scandinavian.

Left: Living room, San Francisco, California, 2019. In the living room, copper cabinets and custom brass sconces are part of the library shelves. The custom rug is by Amadi Carpets and was inspired by a vintage Danish pattern and woven with vintage wool in Turkey. The chair and ottoman are vintage Bruno Mathsson.

Above: Living room, off-the-grid cabin in a forest just outside Los Angeles, California, 2019. A vintage Borge Morgensen daybed in the original fabric and a Gregory Parkinson blanket. The ladder, just visible in the next room, leads to the sleeping loft.

Garden room, Berkeley Hills, California, 2016. Jennifer Doebler and Pat Kelly with their daughters, India and Scarlett, in the garden room. The crates used as a coffee table are Commune and were purchased online by the client back in 2008; they are from our first batch, which were made by Alma Allen.

Master bedroom, Berkeley Hills, California, 2016. The closets are Henry Built, the bedside tables are by Commune, the wall sculpture is by Mary Little, the rug is by Christopher Farr, and the bed cover and pillows were made in India by Gregory Parkinson for Commune.

Above: Living room, Santa Monica, California, 2018. This coffee table is by Ido Yoshimoto. The 800-pound table was carved in Inverness from a single piece of old-growth walnut salvaged by Evan Shively in Marshall, California.

Right: Mud room, West Marin, California, 2016.

Left: Off-the-grid cabin, outside Los Angeles, California, 2019. All materials and furnishings for this cabin renovation were transported down a narrow two-mile canyon path by donkeys or with a hand-built wheelbarrow.

Above: Off-the-grid cabin, outside Los Angeles, California, 2019. Detail of a custom cabinet made with redwood salvaged from the cabin's original interior. The decorative marquetry inlay is a ginkgo tree branch with leaves depicting the colors of the seasons.

Above: Ceramic lamps by Sunja Park for Commune, 2018.

Right: Dining room, West Marin, California, 2016. The ceiling is lined with rush mats woven in England, the pendant is by Stephen White, the armchairs are vintage Hans Wegner, and the table was made by Tripp Carpenter in Bolinas.

Above: Master bedroom, West Marin, California, 2017. This tent serves as master bedroom in a family vacation compound in Northern California. The bed is by Ilse Crawford for De La Espada, the bedside tables are vintage Italian by Mario Ceroli, and the lamps are by Victoria Morris for Commune.

Right: Master bathroom, Beverly Hills, California, 2017. Several rooms were combined to create this master bathroom suite. All the tile is custom Malibu Tile, and the chair and ottoman are by George Smith.

38

Previous: Living room, Los Angeles, California, 2015. In a Spanish-Moorish Revival home in Los Feliz, the sofa is custom, in the style of Jean-Michel Frank, and the chairs are 1930s Art Deco with upholstery by Clarence House. The ottomans are by Holly Hunt. The floor lamp is 1960s Stilnovo, and the fireplace screen is by Commune. The rug is jute by Christopher Farr. The coffee table is 1960s Art Deco, and the painting above the mantel is by Tony Smith.

Above: Powder room, Steven Johanknecht's apartment, Los Angeles, California, 2018. Sconces by Michael Anastassiades, faucet by Rohl, photograph on the wall by Nan Goldin.

Right: Kitchen, West Marin, California, 2016. The walnut butcher-block counter at right is custom-made, and the rug is vintage Navajo.

Table lantern for Remains Lighting, 2015.

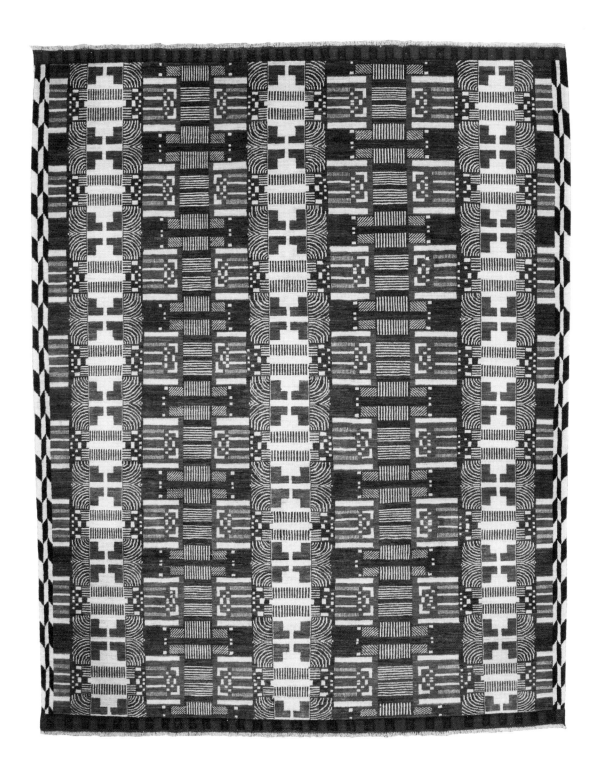

Left: Living room, West Marin, California, 2016.

Above: Klimt rug by Commune for Christopher Farr, 2017.

Following: Kitchen, San Francisco, California, 2019. This fully customized kitchen is handcrafted in salvaged old-growth claro walnut, which was sourced, along with all the other walnut, elm, and redwood used in this project, by Evan Shively at Arborica in Marshall, California. The floor is Spanish black terra-cotta. The counter tops are black polished slate, the backsplash is Nude tile by Heath Ceramics, and the hood is made of copper that is meant to oxidize with age. The pendants are vintage Poul Henningsen, and the stools were made in Brooklyn by Aaron Scaturro.

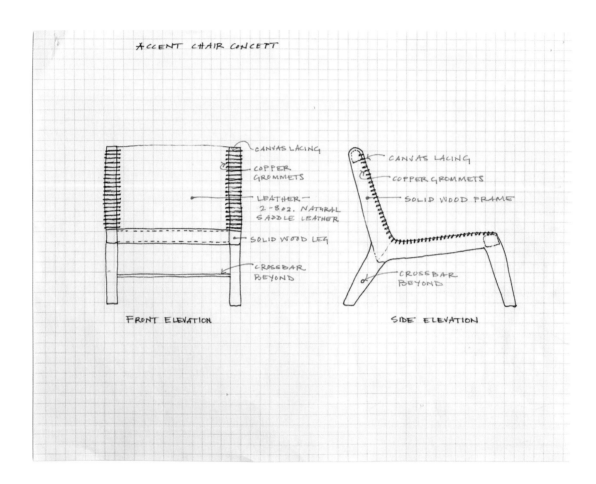

ACCENT CHAIR CONCEPT

FRONT ELEVATION

CANVAS LACING

COPPER GROMMETS

LEATHER —
2-802. NATURAL
SADDLE LEATHER

SOLID WOOD LEG

CROSSBAR BEYOND

SIDE ELEVATION

CANVAS LACING

COPPER GROMMETS

SOLID WOOD FRAME

CROSSBAR BEYOND

Above: Early sketch for Sling chair, part of the Commune collection for West Elm, 2014.

Right: Dining room, Santa Cruz, California, 2019. Arthur Espenet Carpenter's classic wishbone chairs with a trestle table made by his son, Tripp Carpenter, in his father's old workshop in Bolinas.

Following: Living room, Steven Johanknecht's apartment, Los Angeles, California, 2018. The Turkish sofa is by Commune for George Smith, pillows are by Adam Pogue, and the chairs are by Mies van der Rohe and Nanna Ditzel. The rug is vintage Persian.

Above: Living room, Berkeley Hills, California, 2016.

Right: Master bedroom, Steven Johanknecht's apartment, Los Angeles, California, 2018. The vintage dresser is by George Nelson, along with a Robert Mallet-Stevens metal side chair, a 1950s abstract oil painting, and a hand-carved walking stick by Santa Fe folk artist Marshall Girard, son of Alexander Girard.

Left: Model guest room, Ace Hotel Kyoto, Japan, 2020.

Above: Bedroom, Beverly Hills, California, 2017. To bring intimacy to this large master bedroom in a historic Spanish-Colonial Revival home, we chose to paint the ceiling with Pelt by Farrow & Ball. The custom tufted headboard in Clarence House mohair is topped with pillows in fabrics from Schumacher and Pierre Frey. The leather side tables are from BDDW.

54

We have been working with ceramicist Kevin Willis since 2010. There is something Jurassic about his work…like it's from another world. We love his ceramics and his sense of adventure, he's never afraid to try something new. In that spirit he recently added a delicious tequila to his list of creations. La Gritona is distilled by Melly Barajas, a woman in a men's world, in Jalisco, Mexico. We invit you to fill one of Kevin's cups to the bri and toast with us to a new year that w hopefully get us closer to peace a harmony…then have a second one, we are all going to need it.

Our New Year's announcement to vendors and clients, 2019.

Dining room, Berkeley Hills, California, 2017. Our goal was to bring in as much light as possible to this craftsman-style dining room. To reflect light, we used vintage mirrors in the back of the glass cabinets, an old trick from Adolf Loos, and we added a Marthe Armitage wallpaper with a metallic pattern above the redwood paneling. The dining table and sideboard are BDDW, the chairs are by Jas. Becker, and the light fixture is Adolf Loos by Woka Lamps Vienna.

Left: Dining room, Santa Monica, California, 2018. This little bar was inspired by the work of Mathieu Mategot and custom built by Miguel Rojas.

Above: Dining room, Beverly Hills, California, 2017. In this historic Spanish-Colonial Revival home, the dining room is painted with Dinner Party by Benjamin Moore, the dining table is custom in the Art Deco Ruhlmann style, and the nineteenth-century bronze doré chandelier is original to the house. The chairs are by Dessin Fournir, and the rug is antique.

60

Available at
WallpaperSTORE*
See page 147

Within the image:

Entertaining

Punch line

'Big Sur' punchbowl set, by Commune and Kevin Willis

Californian design collective Commune opted to rework a dinner piece that a large group of people could enjoy. Its spin on the typically kitsch punchbowl, ladle and cups is robust and earthy, thanks to ceramicist Kevin Willis' handiwork. The Los Angeles artist cast the shapes out of solid desert clay, and finished with two custom-made, contrasting glazes, giving the set all the makings of a groovy party.

Commune
Founded in 2004, Commune is a modern design studio known for infusing each project that it touches with a cool charm and authenticity. From enigmatic hotel interiors and elegant shopfits to colourful graphic identities and sophisticated homes, the Los Angeles-based studio's talents know few bounds.
communedesign.com

Kevin Willis
Californian artist Kevin Willis spent a large part of his career directing and producing music videos. Despite a couple of Grammy nods, he now pursues painting, ceramics and photography while also running a bar called Cha Cha Lounge in Silver Lake, Los Angeles. He is based at Desert Creek Studios, on the edge of the Mojave Desert.
kevinwillis.biz

PHOTOGRAPHY: BAKER & EVANS WRITER: PEI-RU KEH

Wallpaper* 045

Above: Big Sur punchbowl by Kevin Willis for Commune, featured in *Wallpaper** magazine, 2015.

Right: Channeled side chair by Commune for George Smith, 2016.

Above: Caldera House ski club, Jackson Hole, Wyoming, 2017. In the restaurant are our dining chairs for George Smith and our globe light fixture for Remains Lighting.

Right: Reading nook, West Marin, California, 2016. Oakland, California-based craftsman Kelly Best built the reading nook out of salvaged old-growth redwood sourced from Evan Shively's Arborica in Marshall, California. The redwood stool is by Rick Yoshimoto, who used to assist the legendary sculptor JB Blunk. The pendant is vintage Svend Aage Sørensen.

Left: Master bedroom, Santa Cruz, California, 2019. The table and chairs are by George Nakashima Woodworkers, and the painting is by Terry St. Jean.

Above: Master bathroom, Santa Cruz, California, 2019. The vanity, like all the wall paneling and millwork in the house, is Monterey cypress, with a polished concrete top by Concreteworks in Sausalito. The plumbing fixtures are by Vola, and the sconces are by Dimore Studio. The cabinet hardware is from our own Loop collection for Liz's Antique Hardware.

Left: Off-the-grid cabin, outside Los Angeles, California, 2019. Corner dining area with a built-in banquette and a Hans Wegner chair at a custom oak table. Above the table is an oxidized brass-candle chandelier.

Above: Kitchen, off-the-grid cabin, outside Los Angeles, California, 2019.

Porch, West Marin, California, 2016. A collection of Paolo Soleri wind chimes hang on the porch of the main house in this Northern California vacation compound. The redwood daybed is custom, and the coffee table is by Tripp Carpenter. The chairs are vintage Walter Lamb. The sconces are by Robert Lewis.

GENESIS

Mayer Rus: You two met at Barneys in its heyday in the 1980s and early '90s, when life in retail—and in New York—was quite different.

Roman Alonso: I started out working in New York for a couple of years for the magazines *Connoisseur* and then *Mirabella*. While I was at *Connoisseur*, I used to freelance at Barneys because I wanted to be there more than anything. I was obsessed with it before I even went to college. In high school, I used to read *Interview* and *Details*, so I knew the Barneys ads, I knew what Barneys was. While I was at *Mirabella*, a job opened up at Barneys in the PR department, and I got it. This was in '90.

MR: Steven, how did you get to Barneys?

Steven Johanknecht: I was working at Bergdorf Goodman, and I got to know Richard Lambertson, who worked for Geoffrey Beene at the time. We met when I was doing a Geoffrey Beene installation at Bergdorf's. Richard told Mallory Andrews [at Barneys] about me, and she hired me to do the window displays and store design. I got there probably in 1984. They were just breaking ground for the women's store, and it was Peter Marino's first retail store. Andrée Putman was doing the staircase, the cosmetics area, the shoe department, and the jewelry area, which had those incredible aquariums. That was her idea. I also worked with her on a mannequin, and we introduced her to Ralph Pucci for sculpting it. It was like a Brancusi, and the poses all looked like her. It had huge shoulders and it was impossible to get a jacket on it.

MR: Andrée Putman and Peter Marino—I'd call that the deep end of the pool. This was obviously the pre-leather era for Peter Marino.

RA: Definitely pre-leather. When Barneys started to expand, Peter Marino did ninety percent of the new stores, so we spent a lot of time with him and his staff.

MR: If I can remember clearly through the haze of booze and drugs, the '80s were pretty heady times. Of all the super-glam parties and events Barneys hosted, was there one that epitomized the go-go days?

RA: It had to be the opening of the uptown store on 61st Street and Madison in 1993. The party had no budget. We don't even know how much money we spent on it.

SJ: We could spend whatever we needed to on certain projects. Peter Marino would say, "Let's do these nickel vitrines in Germany with mother-of-pearl inlay," and everybody would be like, "Sure. That sounds great."

RA: We worked on the opening party for almost two years.
On the third floor of the new store, there was a secret door in a closet that led to the grand ballroom of the Pierre Hotel. They'd found this crazy passageway during construction, and Mallory decided to keep it open for use during the opening. Cocktails in a new Peter Marino store was exciting enough, but this . . .

SJ: The invitations were engraved by Mrs. John L. Strong, and they were hand delivered. God knows how much they cost.

RA: At some point in the party, a bunch of us were sent out to collect VIPs, bring them to the party, and escort them through that closet door into the Pierre where the more exclusive party was. We rented every single ballroom at the Pierre, and we filled them with vintage furniture we'd been collecting and reupholstering for more than a year. All these plans were top, top secret. We couldn't even tell our friends.

SJ: We hired Johnny Dynell, who was always the DJ because he was part of the Barneys family, and then the big surprise was Barry White and the Love Unlimited Orchestra, which was a 36-piece orchestra, including a white grand piano. We had to dress all the musicians in white dinner jackets. Then there was a moment when Taylor Dane came up out of the audience to sing "Can't Get Enough of Your Love" with Barry White. We dressed her in Donna Karan. It felt spontaneous, but of course it was all planned.

RA: The setup was all open seating, like a supper club.
I remember Joan Rivers and Hubert de Givenchy left the party because they couldn't sit in the VIP section, which didn't exist. It was all VIP, but they didn't get it.

SJ: Don't forget the cigarette girls who walked around and gave people candy and Nat Sherman cigarettes in custom-made blue velvet boxes.

RA: It was such a funny time. On the one hand, money was pouring out for events like the opening party, but in other areas we'd have to find ways to do things smartly and economically but still make it really cool. At one point, Stephen Sprouse did a little capsule collection of ten jersey dresses, and [Barneys head] Gene Pressman came up to me and said, "You have $5,000 dollars for this party." So I told Sprouse we had no money. And he said, "I've always wanted a slushie machine at a party." I thought that sounded great, so we spent pretty much all the money on two slushie machines and served vodka slushie drinks. Stephen got Naomi Campbell, Kate Moss, and Michele Hicks to model the dresses for free.

SJ: The display department stole two shopping carts from a supermarket in New Jersey. We lined them in black garbage bags and served beer out of them. It was kind of punk chic, but that was Barneys—making magic with a garbage bag.

MR: These stories are really taking me back. Didn't Tom Sachs work in the display department before he became a superstar artist?

SJ: Yes. He made lots of furniture and fixtures for us. He also did those incredible fixtures for the Azzedine Alaïa section at the store uptown, all made out of pennies welded together. They were genius. I wonder where they are now, because they must be worth a fortune.

RA: One year [1994] Tom Sachs made a nativity scene for the Barneys Christmas windows. It depicted the Virgin Mary as Hello Kitty dressed like Madonna. The Three Wise Men were versions of Bart Simpson. The manger had a McDonald's "M" on it, so it was a commentary on the commercialization of Christmas, and it was actually brilliant. Somehow, it came to the attention of an evangelical Christian radio personality, and he went on the air crying blasphemy. This guy had a big following, and people just went nuts. There were picket lines. When the bomb threats started coming in, that was the moment when I thought, "I can't do this anymore."

MR: That's a good transition to your post-Barneys lives. Steven, you eventually left and went to work for William Sofield, right?

SJ: I was with Sofield for two or three years, not very long. Those were the Tom Ford Gucci years. It was a deep immersion in luxury—residential, commercial, hospitality. Bill has an incredible eye, so I learned a lot. But we were definitely not using shopping carts and garbage bags.

MR: Roman, you went to work for Isaac Mizrahi. What was your big takeaway from the Isaac years?

SJ: That pink and red go together?

RA: [laughs] I was there for about four years, and yes, I did learn a lot about color. I think I'm fairly confident with color today, and it has a lot to do with Isaac, because he would challenge us. He loved hot pink, loved it, and he wanted it in almost everything. Whenever anyone questioned it, he'd say, "Tell me one color that does not go with hot pink? Hot pink is a neutral!" He taught me to see the nuance of color, not just the color itself.

MR: So both of you eventually relocated to the West Coast. Did the idea of Commune slowly bubble up over the years?

RA: Not at all. I don't think anyone participating in the birth of Commune had ever thought about it until a particular moment in 2003, when all of us came together and looked at the possibility of creating something new. For Steven and me, this was a chance to work together in the way that we really liked to work. After Barneys, through all these other jobs, we always wanted to get back to that way of doing things, where the team—whether they were in advertising, display, store design, PR, or events—looked at everything together. It was truly holistic, and that's always been our process.

SJ: Definitely. Because of the Barneys experience, we liked working on different kinds of projects, with no hierarchies and in different styles. And from a design perspective, we were thinking about archetypes like the Eames Studio or the Bauhaus. We wanted our company to work on hotels and restaurants, or on branding, and to have graphic design and exhibition design involved, and of course residential interiors, too. We wanted to bring a critical design eye to a lot of different types of projects.

RA: I think there is a lot of precedent for that, obviously, and from the beginning there were opportunities. I had a friend who was starting a little jeans outpost on Beverly Boulevard, Hollywood Trading Company, and he needed a store designed and needed packaging and a graphic identity. These were the kinds of projects we wanted to tackle. We brought in Doug Lloyd, whom we had worked with at Barneys, to do all the packaging and the identity, and then we did the interior.

SJ: Early on, Stila Cosmetics contacted me because they wanted a creative director for stores and packaging and all this other stuff. I figured we could do it as Commune. We worked with them for three or four years, revamping their identity and developing new retail concepts.

RA: It was Stila founder Jeanine Lobell who hired us. We knew her from Barneys where we had launched Stila back in the '90s.

SJ: So many people and projects have a way of connecting back to Barneys. That was our grade school, our finishing school, and our graduate studies. It set the tone for how we like to work and what we like to work on. There's a lot of that Barneys DNA in Commune.

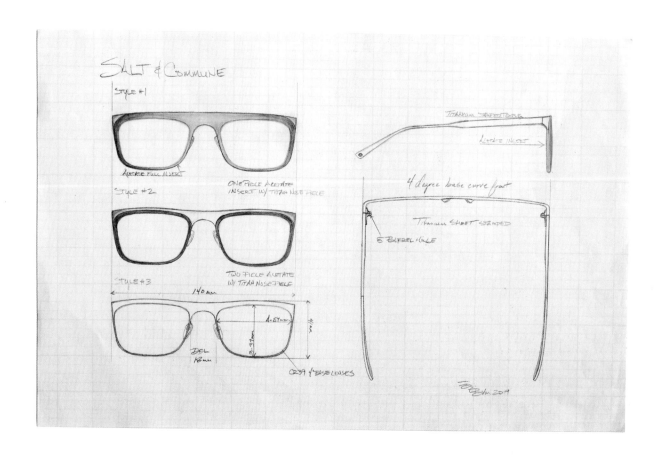

Previous: Board room, Santa Cruz, California, 2019. We collaborated with Feldman Architecture on the design of this beach house. The owner is an avid surfer and wanted a custom "board room" for his surfing equipment. The room opens with an automatic door directly into the interior courtyard. The bar comes in handy for entertaining.

Above: Sketches for our collaboration with Salt Optics, California, 2020.

Right: The Durham Hotel, Durham, North Carolina, 2015. The porte cochere of this hotel is paved with our Malmo tile for Exquisite Surfaces. The newsstand and shoeshine is polished stainless steel.

Japan meets California: Commune created a sencha tea mix in collaboration with Susumuya Tea Shop in Kagoshima, Japan, 2018.

Left: Roman Alonso's apartment, Los Angeles, California, 2018. The airbrushed frieze is by Louis Eisner, the daybed is by Commune, pillows are by Adam Pogue, the stool is by Hideki Takayama, the red chair is vintage Hans Wegner, and the Akari light sculpture is by Isamu Noguchi.

Above: Dome pendant for Remains Lighting, 2015.

82

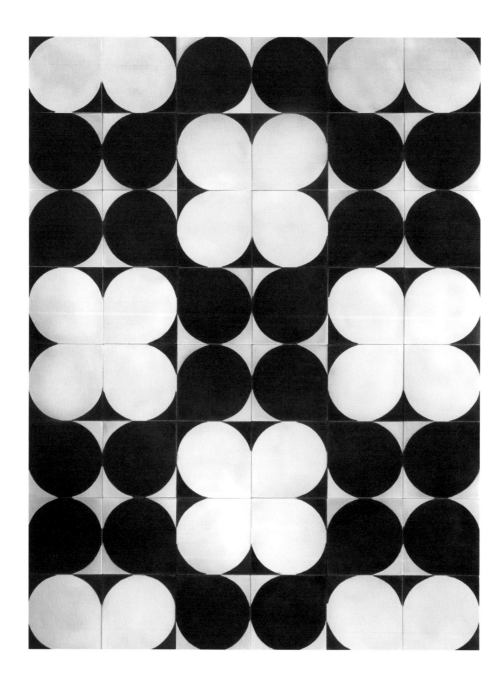

Above: Circle Drop cement tiles for Exquisite Surfaces, 2019.

Right: Ace Hotel Chicago, Illinois, 2015. In the lobby lounge, the I-beam steel table is custom, and the red Plank chairs are by Michael Boyd.

Above: *Home Love* doormat, 2014.

Right: The Durham Hotel, Durham, North Carolina, 2015.

Following: Living room, Paris, France, 2016. This pied-à-terre is in an artist garret with a staircase inspired by Robert Mallet-Stevens, a light fixture by Lindsey Adelman, rug by Christopher Farr, coffee table by Alma Allen, and a sculpture by Adam Silverman.

Above: Dressing room, Beverly Hills, California, 2017. This room in a historic Spanish-Moorish Revival home is lined in custom oak closets. The vanity and mirror are vintage, and the wool and silk carpet is custom.

Right: Master suite at Caldera House ski club, Jackson Hole, Wyoming, 2017. In the master bedroom of the Newberry Suite, the headboard and bedside tables are by George Nakashima Woodworkers, and the sofa is vintage Danish and upholstered in shearling.

Ace Hotel Kyoto, Japan, 2020. This rendering of the main restaurant in the manga style is by Louis Eisner.

Above: Tartine Manufactory, San Francisco, California, 2016. Tartine's first manufactory concept, located in the Heath Factory Building, was inspired by Stickley furniture, Japanese teahouses, Danish cafes, and Alpine lodges.

Right: The Durham Hotel, Durham, North Carolina, 2015. The carpet in the lobby was inspired by the work of Anni Albers. Mica chandeliers by Robert Lewis were inspired by the Okura Hotel in Tokyo.

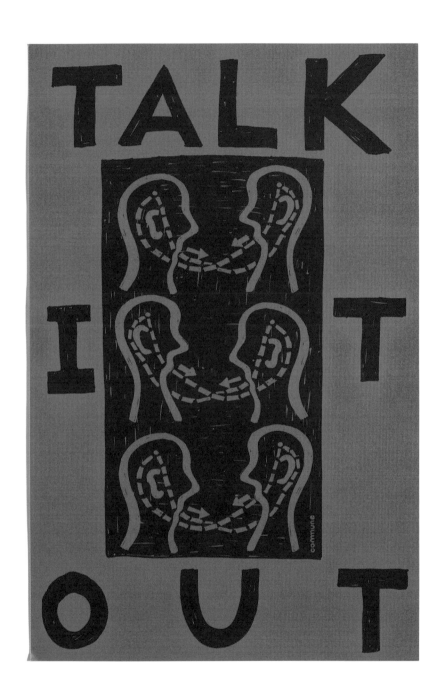

Left: Study, Los Angeles, California, 2017.

Above: Our *Talk It Out* political poster for Paperchase, 2017.

Left: Roman Alonso's apartment, Los Angeles, California, 2018. The dining room furniture is by Michael Boyd, the curtains are by Adam Pogue, and the Globe pendant is by Commune for Remains Lighting. The cabinet is vintage Paul McCobb, refinished in gray; the ceramic bird sculpture is vintage Livia Gorka from the 1960s; and the screen prints are vintage Cuban by Fremez and Amelia Pelaez.

Above: Ace Hotel Downtown Los Angeles, California, 2014. Sketch for a stained glass window that was inspired by a classic Gothic pattern and created by Judson Studios.

Above: The Durham Hotel, Durham, North Carolina, 2015. The bedcovers are by Raleigh Denim and were inspired by Anni Albers.

Right: Roman Alonso's apartment, Los Angeles, California, 2018. An Adam Pogue linen and velvet quilt hangs in the doorway as a room divider. The photographic collage is by Lisa Eisner. The wood sculpture is by Hideki Takayama.

Arrow fire screen, 2013.

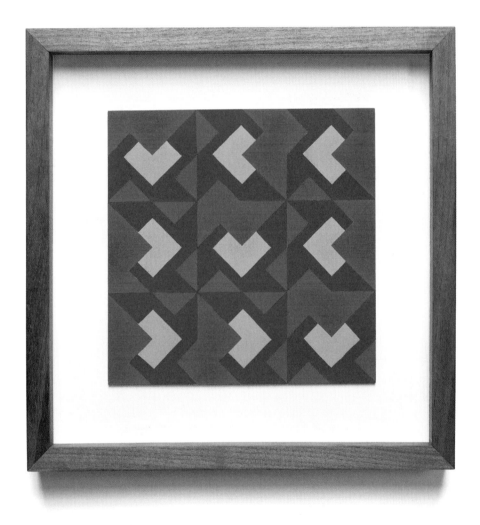

Steven Johanknecht did this painting in 1979. It inspired our Arrow pattern, which we've used on rugs and fire screens.

Children's room, Santa Cruz, California, 2019. The custom beds have headboards upholstered in the Notturno pattern by Josef Frank. The rug is by Christopher Farr. The paintings are by the children, who were inspired by the room and its surroundings.

love and joy from **kori girard** and **commune** 2018

Above: New Year's poster, 2018. Kori Girard did this painting for us. Wishing for an upbeat new year, we sent it out to everyone we knew.

Right: Mud room, Berkeley Hills, California, 2017. Vivienne Westwood wallpaper, Alvar Aalto pendant light, and painted floors by Willem Racke.

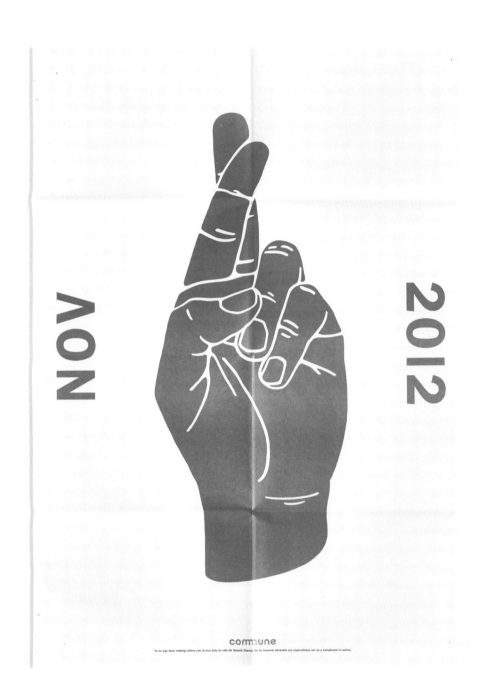

Left: Master bathroom, Paris, France, 2016.

Above: Our poster in support of Barack Obama's re-election campaign, 2012.

Above: Farmer's market stand, Los Angeles, California, 2018. We designed this market stand, made of alder wood and canvas, for the gluten-free bakery Breadblok. When disassembled, it fits in a small van and can be reassembled by two people in less than twenty minutes. The table cloth is by Adam Pogue.

Right: Children's bathroom, Santa Cruz, California, 2019. A custom tile pattern lines the floor and walls. The sconce is Branch by Rich Brilliant Willing, and the pendant is by Areti.

110

Above: Commune for West Elm in *Architectural Digest,* **2016.**

Right: Globe pendant for Remains Lighting, 2017.

LEARNING TO LOVE IN 2007

Lie down on your back, hold your partner's hand a While soft music is played, become aware of yours breathing, and breathe evenly and naturally. Be aw hand, and his feelings.

Now you are limp on the floor, keep your eyes closed and let your partner lift your limp arms and legs, setting them down again carefully.

Next let him hold your head in hands, slowly rotating your head fr side to side, keep your eyes clos trust him, relax.

WWW.COMMUNESITE.COM   666 N. Robertson Blvd. Suite 1 Los Angeles CA 90069 Ph. 310

New Year's poster, 2007.

Face your partner and look into his face, place your hands together, palm to palm, no talking, use palm pressure to feel his warmth.

Roll into a ball on the floor, your partner touches, gently massages, and slowly unwinds the human ball. This is symbolic of release, of letting go.

Sit face to face without talking, with one finger exchange tracing your partner's face, convey warmth to him. Now think as you trace, of a sentence about the other person, how you feel about him as you trace him. Stop tracing and express the sentences.

Sit forehead to forehead with your hands on the shoulders of your partner, close your eyes and dream something about him for three minutes, use one more minute to bring the dream to a close. Share the dream with him.

commune

IMAGE THERAPY • INTERIORS • RETAIL DESIGN • BRANDING • PACKAGING • PRODUCTION DESIGN

Super Choc-o-Food, 2015. Chocolate bars we created in collaboration with Valerie Confections, with Adam and Eve letterpress collectible cards.

CHOCOLATE IS A DIVINE, CELESTIAL DRINK, THE SWEAT OF THE STARS, THE VITAL SEED, DIVINE NECTAR, THE DRINK OF THE GODS, PANACEA AND UNIVERSAL MEDICINE

Entrance hall, Los Angeles, California, 2016. The credenza by Chris Lehrecke and Gabriella Kiss is under a painting by Terry Winters. The turquoise-colored perforated Plank chair is by Michael Boyd. In this historic Spanish-Moorish Revival house by Stiles O. Clements, the paintings are by Ken Price, the custom runner is by Patterson Flynn and Martin, and the drop sculpture on the landing is by Anish Kapoor.

Left: Balcony, Beverly Hills, California, 2017. The vintage rattan chairs are upholstered in fabric from Perennials. Kevin Willis pottery is on a root-wood table, and the wall sculpture is by Curtis Jere.

Above: Our Cactus Flower pattern in Ruby for Christopher Farr Cloth, 2016.

Following: Courtyard, Beverly Hills, California, 2016. The floor tiles in the entry courtyard of this 1927 Spanish-Moorish Revival house are custom by Malibu Tile. The furniture is by Janus et Cie, the white Thumb Pots are by Stan Bitters, and the light fixtures are original to the house.

CALIFORNIA

Mayer Rus: In the past two decades, LA has emerged as a major hub of global culture. In my mind, Commune has been a catalyst in the city's metamorphosis. Is it correct to say that the firm has a California state of mind?

Steven Johanknecht: Yes, we are completely influenced by this place. We always say that Commune couldn't have happened anywhere else. We could not have founded this kind of company in New York. It's somehow more rigid there. Everyone stays in their lane.

Roman Alonso: Nobody here batted an eyelash when we said, "We're starting this company and we're going to do residential and commercial, houses and hotels, graphic design and products—basically we're going to do it all." When we told people in New York, a lot of them didn't understand. They kept saying, "What is it that you do?"

SJ: People actually said, "How can you do hotels and residences? That's not a thing."

RA: Fifteen years ago it was an anomaly to do residential and commercial work—and be equally committed to both—as a studio. Forget about the graphics and brand management, the chocolates, and all the other stuff we did at the beginning. Now, I think the multidisciplinary, integrated approach is more common.

MR: How would you describe the shift in LA's culture and the popular perception of the city since you arrived in the late '90s?

SJ: It used to be all about Hollywood and surfers. Those were the main touchstones for a lot of people. But I think it's become much more than that. People are beginning to understand that the lifestyle that was incubated here over the last century is perhaps more relevant today. Especially for younger people. California nurtured the idea of casual elegant living. The relationship to nature and the outdoors changed how people dressed, ate, entertained, and simply lived in their homes.

RA: Before I moved here, people would tell me, "Don't do it. You're going to suffer a creative death. There's no culture there." That was the standard line, and even if it wasn't true, the fact is that LA used to be much more of an industry town. If you didn't belong to the entertainment world, nobody talked to you. Now there's a lot more of everything here. I think that has a lot to do with the migration of artists, designers, and other creative people wanting to work here. People have always seen California as a place of opportunity, a place of dreams and counterculture and freedom. Somehow, it's managed to perpetuate that image.

MR: Were you always attracted to California?

SJ: Yes! Growing up in Upstate New York, where it was just gray all the time and snowing half the year or raining or humid, I kept thinking, "Look! They're having so much more fun in sunny California." I really didn't visit until I was an adult and working, but I always looked for the opportunity to live here. I loved New York and all that, and I valued the education I got there, but I still wanted to have a different experience. And that's why I jumped at the chance, after twenty years in New York, to take a job with the Gap in San Francisco.

RA: I had zero interest in California my whole life. Since I was a child, I had only ever wanted to live in New York. That was the goal. I was always going to be a New Yorker, and I had no interest in leaving. California was an interesting place to go to for a couple of days of work, but I couldn't wait to get back to New York. But then New York started changing in the late '90s, and I decided I couldn't do the work that I was doing there anymore, and Mizrahi closed, and the person who sang the siren song of Los Angeles for me was Lisa Eisner. She's responsible for my being here. She sold me on it.

MR: From the very beginning, Commune seemed to have a California soul, in terms of philosophy, the embrace of the California craft tradition, the kinds of jobs you were doing. You seemed blissfully unshackled by received ideas about how things should be.

RA: We were starting new lives here, and we were starting to figure out what felt right and what worked. I think it happens very naturally. You start falling in love with a place and you learn what the light calls for, what the weather calls for, what the nature calls for. LA really informed everything we did—materials, color, all of it.

SJ: You pay attention to things differently when you're in a new place. It was the same thing in my early days in New York, working with people like Peter Marino and Andrée Putman. I was just absorbing everything like a sponge. So, many years later, I'm out here and I'm paying attention differently, concentrating differently.

RA: Out here there was this sense of discovery, like, "Oh wow, Stan Bitters, he's so cool. Okay, we're working with him." I think for both of us it's always been about discovering what people we could bring into the mix. That's the essence of Commune.

MR: As LA has become so popular in recent years, and all the starchitects—Herzog & de Meuron, Renzo Piano, Peter Zumthor—have rolled into town, and all the fancy New York and European art galleries have opened an outpost here, do you think there's a danger of LA losing some of its heart and soul?

RA: You definitely see the same socioeconomic forces that have reshaped places like New York and London percolating here. But LA is so big and has so many pockets, it's like a group of villages. I think that many of those villages will hold onto their character for a long time, if for no other reason than geography. Everything is just so spread out. For me, New York has really flattened. You need to have the right mix of people from all walks of life for a city to be a vibrant, creative place. LA has held out so far. San Francisco not so much. I think San Francisco, like New York, is just more limiting in terms of its geography. Wide open space helps.

MR: Speaking of San Francisco, let's talk about Northern California, which has its own design traditions and mythology. Talk to me about working in places like Marin and Napa.

RA: I spent time exploring up there with Lisa [Eisner]. She introduced us to a lot of great things and people up there because she's an explorer and a lover of California. The first time I heard of Heath Ceramics was from her, and it was during our early work with Heath that I began to understand the depth of the California craft movement. Commune has done projects for clients like Heath and Farmshop in both LA and San Francisco, and they're really different. The soul up there isn't the same as the soul in LA.

SJ: The climate difference definitely affects the character of the work we do, especially in the residential jobs. In Southern California you have a lot of the Spanish influence in design and the relationship to the outdoors. Again, I think it all comes down to the architecture, the materials, the colors, and the textures. Different needs stem from a different climate.

RA: Also, I think the clients up north see things a little differently. It's a more pragmatic outlook, a bit more real, maybe because Hollywood isn't there pushing its fantasies.

MR: Do your hospitality clients ever specifically say, "We want this to feel and look like California"?

RA: I think we get hired sometimes because of that, because we have a reputation as champions of California design.

SJ: And sometimes we have to intentionally play against some artificial idea of what California means to people. We don't want to be doing some kind of cartoony schtick. We try to celebrate California in all of its diversity and strangeness.

Previous: Model guest room, Ace Hotel Kyoto, Japan, 2020.

Left: Playroom, San Francisco, California, 2019. A Finn Juhl Pelican chair in a fabric by Kvadrat on an Anni Albers rug by Christopher Farr.

Above: Den, Steven Johanknecht's apartment, Los Angeles, California, 2018. The Finn Juhl chair drawings are from a trip to the Finn Juhl house outside Copenhagen, Denmark. The brass lantern is by Commune for Remains Lighting, and the patchwork pillow is by Adam Pogue.

Left: Family room, Beverly Hills, California, 2017. This custom design for a bar was inspired by the furniture of Thomas Molesworth. We changed the color of the pool-table felt to a vivid blue. The Native American motifs on the beams were hand-stenciled by artist Nic Valle. The screen print is Ed Ruscha, and the rug is by Christopher Farr.

Above: Living room, Malibu, California, 2014. No job is ever too small if it's interesting to us and poses a challenge. We designed this trailer in Malibu's Paradise Cove for a dear friend of the firm. The sleeping nooks double as sofas and guest beds. The coffee table is by Alma Allen, and the print on the wall is by Mike Mills.

Outdoor living room, San Francisco, California, 2019. This 5,000-square-foot home was designed in collaboration with Feldman Architecture. It was inspired by modernist Scandinavian houses and was literally hand-built by Forsythe General Contractors. The limewashed Norman brick exterior walls wrap into the interior, and the black terra-cotta floors and plaster ceilings from inside the house spill out to this courtyard through large folding doors in the kitchen, creating a fully indoor/outdoor living area. The ceramic fireplace is by Stan Bitters, and the Cherry Bomb light fixture is by Lindsey Adelman. The lounge furniture is James Perse, with stools by Sunja Park. The dining table is by Lief and the chairs are Vincent Van Duysen for Paola Lenti.

Above: Steven Johanknecht's desk, Los Angeles, California, 2018.

Right: City Mouse restaurant, Ace Hotel Chicago, Illinois, 2016. Behind the host stand is a wall hanging that was hand-woven in Oaxaca by artist Tanya Aguiñiga. It depicts an aerial view of the buildings along the banks of the Chicago River.

Roman Alonso in his living room, Los Angeles, California, 2018. The patchwork curtains were Adam Pogue's first commission and were meant to resemble stained glass. Roman acquired the Indian rug from a Tony Duquette estate sale. The coffee table was made for him by Michael Boyd, the stools and small sculptures are by Alma Allen, and the table lamp is by ceramicist Adam Silverman. Other works in the room are by Fayad Jamís, Dr. Lakra, Monique Van Genderen, Steven Johanknecht, Billy Sullivan, and Ido Yoshimoto, among others. The sofa is by Commune for George Smith, and the chair is by Pierre Paulin from JF Chen.

Left: Reading nook, Santa Cruz, California, 2019. The painting is by Clare Rojas, and the vintage French stool sits on a rug by Orley Shabahang.

Above: Adam Pogue for Commune carved-foot ottoman, 2015.

A rendering by Konstantin Kakanias of a restaurant in an upcoming museum, Los Angeles, California, 2020.

Left: Living room, Beverly Hills, California, 2017. The client's own plein-air painting collection is mixed with wood carvings, artisan pottery, vintage textiles, and silk velvet.

Above: *Flapper* by Mike Mills, part of a poster series for Commune, 2014.

Left: Roman Alonso's kitchen, Los Angeles, California, 2017. The cabinets are replicas of the originals from 1966 and painted in the colors Manhattan Bridge and Home by Drikolor. All appliances, counters, and the backsplash are stainless steel; the plumbing fixtures are Vola; and the Ribbon cabinet pulls are Commune for Liz's Antique Hardware. The large print is by Sister Corita, and the vintage Fillmore posters are from a collection that was started back in New York in the 1990s. The tractor stool is by Michael Boyd.

Above: Outdoor shower, Malibu, California, 2014.

Above: Powder room, Beverly Hills, California, 2017. This residence is next door to the Beverly Hills Hotel, where the clients are regulars and have a house account. In a nod to their love of the place, we lined the powder room in Don Loper's Martinique wallpaper, which was designed for the hotel in 1942.

Right: Bathroom, Roman Alonso's apartment, Los Angeles, California, 2018. The screen prints are vintage Cuban movie posters from the '60s and '70s.

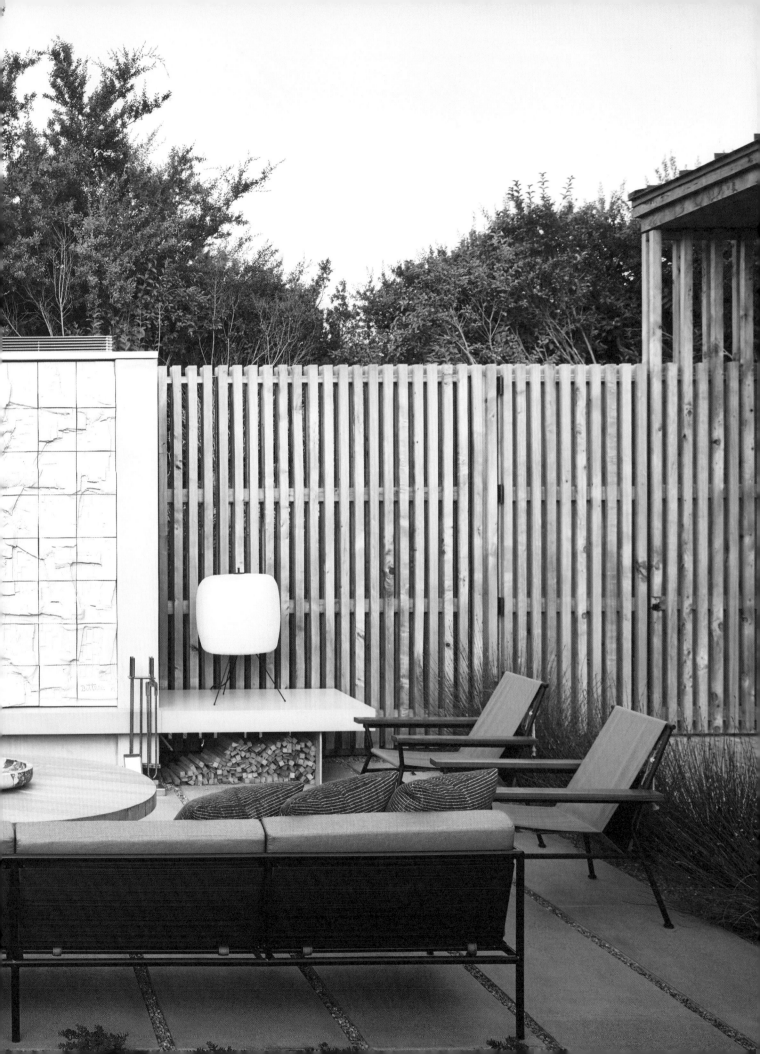

Previous: Interior courtyard, Santa Cruz, California, 2019. The exterior of this beach house is clad in salvaged Monterey cypress sourced by Arborica. It is meant to patina and turn gray with time. The ceramic fireplace is by Stan Bitters; the sofa is by 10Ten; the chairs are Garza Marfa; and the daybed and coffee table are custom made by Miguel Rojas. The tile on the top of the side table is vintage Heath Ceramics.

Left: Model guest room, Ace Hotel Kyoto, Japan, 2020. All the textiles in the guest rooms were created in collaboration with Akira Minagawa of Mina Perhonen. The artwork is by Samiro Yunoki.

Above: Master bedroom, Santa Cruz, California, 2019. The bed was custom made by Miguel Rojas. The bedding is Commune for Hamburg House, and the lamp is by Victoria Morris. The woven wall hanging is by Kira Dominguez Hultgren; it was commissioned by art consultant Allison Harding and incorporates fabric remnants from the dress and dress shirt our clients wore on their first date.

Left: Bathroom, Roman Alonso's apartment, Los Angeles, California, 2017. To maximize storage, the custom vanity was inspired by Japanese tansu cabinets, which incorporate as many drawers, compartments, and cubbyholes as possible, hidden and otherwise. The shower door is custom brass and the plumbing fixtures are Vola. The tile is Heath, and the paint colors are Corbusier, licensed by Drikolor. The light fixture in the vanity is Venini glass.

Above: Kitchen, Roman Alonso's apartment, Los Angeles, California, 2017. The Ribbon pulls are by Commune for Liz's Antique Hardware, and on the counter is a Nancy Pearce for Commune Flared bowl.

Guest room, Santa Cruz, California, 2019. Above: Custom bed by Doug McCollough and a rug by Doris Leslie Blau. Right: The lounge chair is by Estudio Persona, with a vintage African stool and a painting by Zack Harris.

Left: Guest bedroom, West Marin, California, 2016. For the guest rooms at a family vacation compound, we created custom vanities with a hanging bar, hooks, drawers, shelf, bench seat, and mirror. The chair and floor lamp are vintage Danish, and the rug is vintage Swedish from Doris Leslie Blau.

Above: Commune's Plaid for Christopher Farr Cloth, 2016.

Above: Bedroom, West Marin, California, 2016. This tiny bedroom for a teenage girl is lined with Marthe Armitage's Clematis hand-printed wallpaper. The bedside table is custom made by Miguel Rojas, and the rug is vintage Navajo.

Right: Master bedroom, Berkeley Hills, California, 2016. The red goat-hide chair and ottoman are Kaare Klint by Rud. Rasmussen. The stool is Alma Allen, and the lamp is Josef Frank No. 1842 by Svenskt Tenn. The curtain fabric is by Liberty, and the custom handspun wool rug is by Christopher Farr.

Above: Choc-o-Puk by Commune for Valerie Confections, 2017.

Right: Sun room, Berkeley Hills, California, 2016. Bernhard and Poppy hang out on a Commune daybed with pillows by Gregory Parkinson and Adam Pogue. The wood sculptures are by Cargo Kojiro Nomura, and the rug is vintage Turkish.

Following: Living room, Santa Cruz, California, 2019. The interior of this beach house, designed in collaboration with Feldman Architecture, is entirely finished in Monterey cypress and Belgian plaster by Domingue. The rug is by Doris Leslie Blau. The two Rietveld Utrecht chairs (in the foreground) are upholstered in Hermès fabric. The daybed is custom by Classic Design, and the sofa is Vincent Van Duysen for Gubi. The coffee table is by Alma Allen, and the stone top side table is by Michael Boyd. The fireplace screen is a constellation of stars woven in brass wire by Tanya Aguiñiga.

Above: Guest room, Santa Cruz, California, 2019. The walnut custom desk is by Miguel Rojas from a Commune design, the Marolles chair is by Carneros Studios, and our V-Lite sconce is for Atelier de Troupe.

Right: Reading nook, Santa Cruz, California, 2019.

Den, Steven Johanknecht's apartment, Los Angeles, California, 2018. This cozy library-lounge-workspace was created by lining the entire room in oak millwork incorporating shelving, a built-in desk, and a daybed. The framed posters are from a trip to the Bauhaus in Dessau, Germany, and to Sweden.

Bedroom, Steven Johanknecht's apartment, Los Angeles, California, 2018. The walls are painted with Farrow & Ball's Pelt. The citron-colored linen bedcover fabric is Pierre Frey, and the bed and bedside tables are George Nelson. The photograph is by Cindy Sherman, and the Peter Max screen print is from a flea market.

Above: Foyer, Santa Cruz, California, 2019. This entry cabinet is lined in Josef Frank fabric and has Lisa Eisner cast-brass Nugget drawer pulls. The mirror is vintage Italian.

Right: Living room, Santa Cruz, California, 2019. On the daybed is a pillow by Adam Pogue, and on the wall is a painting by Caitlin Lonegan. The floor lamp is vintage Paavo Tynell.

174

Previous: Master bedroom, Santa Cruz, California, 2019.

Off-the grid cabin, outside Los Angeles, California, 2019. Above: The bronze doorknob, produced by Van Cronenburg workshop in Belgium, was cast directly from a river rock found on the cabin site. Right: The working vintage telephone connects to the local pack station. A custom side cabinet was inspired by Gerrit Rietveld.

Following: Off-the-grid cabin, outside Los Angeles, California, 2019.

COLLABORATION

Mayer Rus: The idea of collaboration is obviously built into the name of the firm. What does it mean specifically at Commune?

Roman Alonso: It means that everything we do, we do with others. And with each other. It's not about ego. We're only as good as the team.

Steven Johanknecht: Collaboration means letting designs evolve organically, with the input of clients and everyone in the studio, rather than trying to impose some sort of house style or predetermined solution.

MR: How do you select your artisan and artist collaborators?

SJ: We look for quality in workmanship, of course, and a similar point of view. It's very nuanced, and it's not always the ones people think would be a good fit. We're looking for collaborators who get it, even if it's impossible to explain what *it* is. It's an affinity, a shared way of looking at things.

MR: Let's talk about your most fruitful ongoing relationships. Alma Allen, for one, has been in the Commune fold from the beginning, right?

RA: Well, I remember him from New York in the '90s, when he'd set up in front of the post office on Prince Street in Soho. He'd have these incredible little sculptures displayed on an ironing board. I never got one, but I really wanted one. Then I recognized his stuff at a little store he had in the early 2000s on Abbot Kinney in Venice, where he showed everything from sculptures to furniture. We had just started Commune, and we commissioned him to do a couple of things for Hollywood Trading Company, the jeans store we designed. We also bought his stools for the restaurant Ammo, and from that moment on he's been in every project we've done.

SJ: He did a lot of stuff for the Ace Hotel in Palm Springs. He did a table and stool in every guest room, and the handles on the lobby doors are the first bronze pieces he ever did, I think. He also did the door handles at the Ace Downtown LA.

RA: He always talked about the fact that he was an artist, and we understood him as an artist. We knew that all this furniture that he was producing for us was going to help him continue with his art practice. We felt super lucky—and we made sure that our clients understood how lucky they were. It was always connected.

SJ: We always respect the vision and identity of the people we work with. Regardless of what we're asking them to do, we try to give them the space and the resources to make things they are proud of. I think Alma's really proud of the stuff he's made for our projects.

MR: Tell me about Adam Pogue.

RA: He used to work for Nina Garduno at FreeCity. Nina recognized that he was skilled with fabric and stitching. He'd do patches on the clothing and the blankets she was making. At some point he decided that he didn't want to do that anymore, and he showed me a patchwork quilt he'd made. I told him, "Forget the quilt, we're going to make something else." That's the day I commissioned him to do the incredible curtains in my apartment. I told him I wanted them to feel like stained glass, and he delivered.

SJ: His eye is amazing, and it's always changing, depending on the project. We'll say, "Let's go monochromatic on this, or let's bring these Japanese fabrics into that." Then he'll figure out a way to incorporate them into his pillows, window hangings, and everything else he makes.

RA: In general, we make sure that they are not only happy with what they're doing, but also that their career and their personal work is evolving. People had started asking Adam to do things that weren't right for him, and he didn't know how to say no. I said, "Let us say no for you." And that's how our relationship began evolving into a situation where he's able to make an incredible range of pieces—and they're the right things for him and for us. Adam is the first maker that we officially represented, which means that all commissions and all site-specific work he does comes to Commune, and then we also sell all his product.

MR: Of course, Lisa Eisner has been a collaborator, friend, guiding light, and more from the beginning.

RA: We used to represent her as a photographer when we had Commune Images, and now we make hardware and decorative objects with her. The relationship is always evolving. For the hardware, we went into her rock and arrowhead collection and edited a group that we then cast and made into brass hardware. We also made abalone shell incense holders and now we are making these beautiful sea urchin-like ones. Lisa also really wanted to make these amulets with horsehair tails and other things that she felt had some kind of metaphysical, witchy power. We said, "Sure, let's put them in the Commune online shop and see what happens." Collaborating with people we love and admire gives us a ton of flexibility. We have the freedom to experiment—and to try again when we fail.

Previous: Lobby, Ace Hotel Chicago, Illinois, 2016. Much of our inspiration for this project came from Mies van der Rohe. We brought the white brick on the exterior into the lobby and put in a black terrazzo floor. We installed Homasote and plywood on the ceiling to hide necessary mechanical equipment and to help with acoustics. The rug is by George Nakashima for Edward Fields, and we mixed furniture by Michael Boyd with a few vintage pieces.

Left: Tartine Manufactory, San Francisco, California, 2016.

Above: El Centro Apartments, Hollywood, California, 2018. This exterior common area connects four buildings in the apartment complex. The walkways are imbedded with areas where people can lounge, work, have barbeques, and dine al fresco.

Bedroom, Santa Monica, California, 2018. We worked on this custom bed with Miguel Rojas. The headboard is from an incredible old-growth walnut slab from Evan Shively at Arborica. The light fixture is by Stephen White, and the ceramic sculpture is by Adam Silverman.

Left: Bedroom, Los Angeles, California, 2018. Wing chair designed by Commune for George Smith. *Couples* by Brice Marden (1996) hangs above a dresser by BDDW, and an untitled piece by Anish Kapoor, visible through the doorway, hangs in the stairway.

Above: Goop Lab, New York, New York, 2018. The design of this elliptical room was inspired by the glamourous homes of old Hollywood.

Master bathroom, Santa Monica, California, 2018. The combined steam shower and bathtub is lined in Nude tiles by Heath. The fabric in the shoji screens was hand woven by Hechizoo in Colombia. The rug is by Christopher Farr, and the solid brass mirror is custom.

190

Above: Guest room with bunk beds, Santa Cruz, California, 2019.

Right: Living room, San Francisco, California, 2019. In this corner of the room, we combined Hans Wegner Circle chairs with a Kieran Kinsella walnut stool and an Isamu Noguchi Akari light sculpture.

Guest room, Ace Hotel Chicago, Illinois, 2016.

Above: Victoria Morris for Commune Carved bowl, 2015.

Right: Guest room, San Francisco, California, 2019. A BDDW Mills bed is upholstered in a custom Hechizoo fabric, and a Sunja Park ceramic lamp sits on a George Nakashima Woodworkers Swett nightstand.

Following: Living room, Santa Monica, California, 2018. This apartment in an iconic 1960s building has a spectacular view of the coast all the way up to Malibu. The client wanted us to "bring in the view," so we painted the room in a combination of colors that were inspired by Le Corbusier's palette for his Maison La Roche in the south of France. Artist Louis Eisner painted the wall mural in these colors with acrylic paint.

Above: Bar, The Durham Hotel, Durham, North Carolina, 2015.

Right: Bedroom, Santa Monica, California, 2018.

Dining room, Santa Monica, California, 2018. We designed the brass boxes on the ceiling with lighting designer Sean O'Connor. The fixture on the wall is a Cherry Bomb wall sconce by Lindsey Adelman. The dining table is by Miguel Rojas and was inspired by Charlotte Perriand, the chairs are by George Nakashima Woodworkers, and the hand-woven rug is by Hechizoo.

Living room, Steven Johanknecht's apartment, Los Angeles, California, 2018. The painting of a shipwreck was a gift from Steven's grandmother, and it hangs above a vintage zebrawood credenza by Knoll. The light blue vase is a collaboration between Adam Silverman and Alma Allen, organized by Commune for Heath; the patchwork pillow is by Adam Pogue.

Above: Bedroom, Los Angeles, California, 2016. This master bedroom is in a historic Spanish-Moorish Revival house by Stiles O. Clements. Paint color and furnishings were selected to enhance the painted ceiling, which was original to the house. Commune designed the chairs for George Smith, but the side table is by Gio Ponti. Above the custom headboard, upholstered in blue horsehair, hangs *...and warmth once again floods the earth* by Darren Almond (2014).

Right: Bedroom, Santa Monica, California, 2018. The Vladimir Kagan chair and ottoman are paired with an Alma Allen sugar-pine stool. The painting is by Steven Johanknecht.

Left: Dressing room, San Francisco, California, 2019.

Above: Master bathroom, San Francisco, California, 2019. Limestone slab floors and walls are paired with a claro walnut and concrete custom vanity. The faucets are Henry by Waterworks. Our Globe pendant for Remains Lighting hangs above.

Above: A collection of ceramic lamps and vases made for Commune by Victoria Morris, Sunja Park, and Kevin Willis, 2018.

Right: Club lounge, Caldera House ski club, Jackson Hole, Wyoming, 2017. The club chairs were inspired by a chair we noticed in a photo of the late furniture designer Thomas Molesworth's house.

Club lounge, Caldera House ski club, Jackson Hole, Wyoming, 2017. Vintage Scandinavian furnishings mix with our Turkish sofa for George Smith and a Prouvé chair by Cassina (background, far right).

City Mouse restaurant lounge, Ace Hotel Chicago, Illinois, 2018.

El Centro Apartments, Hollywood, California, 2018. Communal living area in the heart of Los Angeles. The custom sofa is Commune for George Smith, and the wall installation is by Bradley Duncan.

Left: Kitchen, Santa Monica, California, 2018. The walnut bench, table, and stool are custom, and the pendant is a vintage Vilhelm Lauritzen for Louis Poulsen. The door hardware is custom by Van Cronenburg.

Above: Kitchen, Santa Monica, California, 2018. This custom kitchen has solid oak cabinets painted in Le Corbusier Blanche white. For the countertop, we laid a heavy-gauge stainless steel layer, with integrated sinks, on top of solid oak. The sliders above the sink are heavy-gauge aluminum sheets, and the stove backsplash and hood are copper. The backsplash tile is Nude unglazed tile by Heath, and the plumbing fixtures are by Waterworks.

Left: Entry foyer and dining room, San Francisco, California, 2019. The rug is Commune for Christopher Farr and the painting is by Nanno de Groot.

Above: Dining room, San Francisco, California, 2019. The stair treads are local elm planks, and the cabinets are reclaimed old-growth claro walnut.

Off-the-grid cabin, outside Los Angeles, California, 2019. Japanese inspired sleeping loft with grass-cloth walls and ceiling with a hardwood floor. We wanted to create a cozy Zen space with an emphasis on textures, warm materials, and soft bedding.

Above: Breadblok bakery, Santa Monica, California, 2020.

Right: Master bedroom, San Francisco, California, 2019.

Master bathroom, Santa Monica, California, 2018. This custom vanity has Nugget drawer pulls by Lisa Eisner for Commune. The plumbing fixtures are Henry by Waterworks, and the sconces are Branch by Rich Brilliant Willing. The mirrors are a Gio Ponti design.

Goop Lab, New York, New York, 2018. Jewelry area in the brand's flagship store, featuring silver-stained tambour wood millwork and brass trim. The hand-painted frieze is by artist Louis Eisner.

Goop Lab, New York, New York, 2018. There is a functional kitchen area in the rear of the store.

Back deck, Santa Cruz, California, 2019.

OBJECT LESSON

Mayer Rus: We were just talking about collaborations with particular artists and artisans. Let's discuss the product lines that Commune creates with and for other companies. And there are many.

Steven Johanknecht: We've done carpets and fabric for Christopher Farr, furniture for George Smith, tiles for Exquisite Surfaces, lighting for Remains, hardware for Liz's Antique Hardware, bedding for Hamburg House . . .

MR: You've been busy!

Roman Alonso: And then there's the stuff that falls outside the traditional boundaries of home design—the chocolates with Valerie, room scents with L'Oeil du Vert, tea with Susumuya Tea in Japan, eyewear with Salt.

MR: Let's start with the most delicious. What's the story with the chocolate? How and why did you venture into edible territory?

RA: Like most things, it was out of necessity. We wanted to make gifts for people for New Year's, and it was always a hassle to decide what we should do. Then we figured, "Who doesn't like chocolate?"

SJ: So we connected with our friends Valerie Gordon and Stan Weightman at Valerie Confections, which makes incredible chocolate, and decided to make something together.

RA: We'd have these really fun meetings, sampling different things and cooking up ideas for what would best represent Commune and Valerie. We'd say, "We need to make something round. Can you make a moon pie?" And she'd say, "Why would I want to make a moon pie?" And then we'd deconstruct it and end up with a brown rice cookie filled with macha and dipped in salted chocolate. Not exactly a moon pie.

SJ: And after conceptualizing these different collections, we'd design the packaging and the collateral stuff. These kinds of projects are the most fun, as you might imagine.

MR: What's the eyewear story?

RA: We were approached by Salt in Orange County. They make expensive glasses in Japan. The first thing is, we only make eyeglass frames that we'd both want to wear. Right now, we're doing three different profiles and an eyewear case with a little screwdriver and extra screws and a mechanical pencil in a really, really nice pocket guard.

MR: How did you connect with Remains Lighting?

SJ: I met the founder, David Calligeros, on a trip to Berlin. It's all pretty simple and straightforward when you're working with people who share a similar sensibility about how things should be made and what products are worth making.

RA: Making carpets with Christopher Farr has been an amazing education for us. That's the other part of collaboration, right? Who are we interested in learning from? Early on, Steven and I made a pact that we're not going to design anything that we and our clients wouldn't use.

MR: This is a bit of a pivot, but let's talk about the posters and the mailers.

SJ: The first one we did was in 2006. It was a famous Dennis Stock photograph from the 1970s of an actor driving a Charger at Universal Studios. We thought the image really captured LA and its weirdness. Then we added "2006" to the Goodyear logo on the tire. We sent it out as a New Year's announcement. It helped establish a vibe for us at the moment.

RA: We've done it every year since. Sometimes they have a political message. The first one that had a political bent we did while the war in Iraq was going on, in 2007 maybe, when Bush was president. I had found this poster from the Weather Underground that had an image of a rifle, and it said, "Piece Now." We changed it to "Peace Now," and we had a photographer that we were representing, Bart Cooke, add flowers coming out of the rifle. After that we did ones for Obama and Hillary Clinton.

MR: Do you ever get blowback about the political content?

SJ: We never have. Not once. And we send them to everyone in our database.

RA: We've always strived for honesty, to project exactly who we are. That's the best advertising. Be yourself and you'll attract like-minded people and filter out the rest.

People respect and appreciate openness and self-awareness.
Plus, it's our way of doing our part.

MR: I had my Hillary poster up for almost two years, long
after the election. I couldn't take it down. It was too hard.

SJ: We tried to edit our mailing list once, trying to figure
out which people might not appreciate the message.
And then we were just like, "Nah."

RA: We figured if someone doesn't like it, they can throw
it in the garbage can.

Previous: City Mouse restaurant, Ace Hotel Chicago, Illinois, 2015. In the dining room, the floating banquette was devised to allow for light and reflection throughout the black terrazzo floor. The tables and chairs are our design. The table bases and tops are green Forbo linoleum with brass accents. The chrome tube chairs are upholstered in leather and white Ultrasuede. The graphic door panels in the back are by Chad Kouri.

Above: Guest room bathroom, Ace Hotel Chicago, Illinois, 2015. We incorporated the vanities into the cabinetry and exposed them. The metal pedestals were inspired by the balconies at the Bauhaus in Dessau, Germany. The Bauhaus is a common thread throughout the design of the hotel.

Right: Guest suite, Ace Hotel Chicago, Illinois, 2015.

Above: Guest suite, Ace Hotel Chicago, Illinois, 2015. The stained plywood on the wall was inspired by Mies van der Rohe's love of paneling. The rug is by George Nakashima for Edward Fields, the floor lamp is an Akari light sculpture by Isamu Noguchi, and the furniture is by Michael Boyd.

Right: Waydown rooftop bar, Ace Hotel Chicago, Illinois, 2015. The DJ stand is by artist Steven Haulenbeek and was made of sand left over from metal casting combined with resin. The collage wall panels are by Erik DeBat.

Family room, Santa Monica, California, 2018. The focus of this room is a large television, so comfortable viewing was our goal for the design. The walls are covered in indigo braided wallpaper, and our Turkish sofa for George Smith is covered in Loro Piana denim. The lounge chair (far left) is vintage Hans Wegner, and the custom coffee table holds remotes for the media equipment. The chest (far right) is vintage Chinese and used to belong to our client's grandmother. The custom shoji doors (left wall) are made with woven bamboo imported from Japan; the window panels (right wall) are handwoven by Hechizoo.

Left: Guest bathroom, Santa Cruz, California, 2019. Our Mochi Indigo cement tile for Exquisite Surfaces.

Above: Family room, San Francisco, California, 2019. The custom sofa is upholstered in Anakreon by Josef Frank, and a walnut coffee table carved by Ido Yoshimoto sits on our Plaid rug for Christopher Farr. The floor cushions are by Adam Pogue, and the light fixture is vintage Angelo Lelli for Arredoluce.

Left: Lobby lounge, Ace Hotel Chicago, Illinois, 2015. Vintage furniture mingles with tables by Michael Boyd, who also found the vintage pieces. The woven hanging panel is by Tanya Aguiñiga, and the rug is Edward Fields.

Above: Stumptown Coffee, Chicago, Illinois, 2015. The design for this coffee shop, adjacent to the Ace Hotel, was inspired by the work of Robert Mallet-Stevens. The counters are stainless steel topped with linoleum flooring, and the custom light fixture is brass.

Following: Tartine Manufactory, San Francisco, California, 2015. The concept for this location had to be well integrated into the building façade, which is located in the Heath factory building in what is known as the Dogpatch neighborhood.

Left: Ace Hotel Chicago, Illinois, 2015. For the roof garden of the hotel, we commissioned artist Jonathan Nesci to create a kind of communal hammock-with-dome.

Above: Waydown rooftop bar, Ace Hotel Chicago, Illinois, 2015.

Meditation cabin, West Marin, California, 2016. This simple redwood structure is part of a vacation compound on ten acres north of San Francisco. We painted the interior Yves Klein blue, and added stained glass windows and a tatami platform made of salvaged old-growth redwood. The view from the bed, of Black Mountain and the surrounding hills, is spectacular.

Left: Locker room bathroom, Caldera House ski club, Jackson Hole, Wyoming, 2016.

Above: Off-the-grid cabin, outside Los Angeles, California, 2019. This cedar lined "outhouse" with inset grasscloth has solar panels that provide energy for lighting and heat for the toilet seat.

Following: Living room, San Francisco, California, 2019. This living room opens out to a deck with a magnificent view of the city. The teak lounge chairs are by Carlos Motta, and the custom table was inspired by the work of Clara Porset.

ELEMENTS OF STYLE

Mayer Rus: This is such a tedious question—you can imagine how much more tedious it becomes when you've been asking designers for thirty years—but how would you describe the Commune aesthetic?

Roman Alonso: Steven, you want to give this one a try?

Steven Johanknecht: I'll try to keep the bullshit to a minimum. The Commune aesthetic is honest, personal, well-integrated, layered, thoughtful, and finely crafted. It has a lot to do with our process, which attempts to avoid predetermined results, because you never want too much of one thing or anything too expected. The goal is to create something that lasts over time. It has to feel fresh and current, but it can't just be an Instagrammable moment.

RA: It's not about us. It's about the clients. So if there's a hallmark in our work, it's about making it feel as personal to them as possible. People's identities and personalities are layered, so their interiors have to be just as layered. It's about conjuring a physical manifestation of something extremely personal, an emotion, a desire, a dream.

SJ: Sometimes a client comes to us and they want a particular thing that ultimately is not really them. So part of the process is helping them discover who they really are and what they love. With every project, there's a different life, a different lifestyle, different needs, and we try to make it as specific and true to that client as possible.

RA: There are definitely certain things and ideas that we return to, and sometimes I feel like, "Oh god, I'm using that again, it's so of the moment." But if something is well-designed and has a certain level of quality, maybe that's not a problem. Twenty years from now I'm going be happy I made that choice because this thing is going to be around, and be beautiful, forever.

SJ: The goal is to create something sustainable and timeless, something the client won't feel compelled to switch out in five years.

RA: I'm always thinking about the waste, the piles of garbage that our business can create. My parents had the same furniture from the time I was born until I was thirteen years old, and it only changed because we had to leave Venezuela and move to Miami. My mom would reupholster the furniture, and a couple of times she redid the wallpaper, but that was it. The furniture stayed the same.

MR: Even while you're reaching for something that will stand the test of time, do you feel like you still need to be searching for the next big thing?

SJ: Not really. It's important to remain relevant and to know what's out there, but for us, it's not about staying on top of trends and what's happening next. The most important thing is what feels right. We never want to find ourselves trying to channel some perceived, artificial sense of the zeitgeist.

MR: I think your Instagram is a very precise distillation of the Commune ethos. Who does it?

RA: I do. We tried at the beginning to have our public relations team do it. Mickey Boardman from *Paper* came up to me at a party in New York and said, "Your Instagram sucks!," and I have to thank him for that, because it was true. It was fucking horrible. So I went back, deleted all of it, and started fresh. It's actually kind of enjoyable. I think everything that we put out has to have a genuine personality, whether it's ours or somebody else's. It has to reflect who we, as a collective group, believe we are.

Previous: Guest suite, Caldera House ski club, Jackson Hole, Wyoming, 2016. In the Taupo Suite, we combined Alpine sophistication with the warmth and comfort of the American West. The rug is a Swedish pattern custom woven in Turkey. The sofas are Vincent Van Duysen for Gubi, and the chairs are Hans Wegner and Axel Vervoordt. The floor lamp is BDDW, and the table lamps are by Adam Silverman.

Above: Reception, Ace Hotel Chicago, Illinois, 2016. The Christy Matson woven wall hanging was inspired by the work of Anni Albers, and the ceramic sconces are by Adam Silverman.

Right: Locker room, Caldera House ski club, Jackson Hole, Wyoming, 2016.

Breadblok bakery, Santa Monica, California, 2020. For this gluten-free bakery, the client wanted to celebrate her family's roots in Provence, but with a decidedly Californian vibe. We laid down a Saltillo tile floor and covered the walls in plaster by Domingue and designed a monumental travertine counter that extends the length of the space and holds baked goods, pastries, cash wrap, and espresso maker. The pendant light fixtures were handwoven by Dax Savage and the parchment sconces are by Fernando Santangelo.

Left: Guest suite, Caldera House ski club, Jackson Hole, Wyoming, 2016. Roman travertine lines the master bath in the Newberry Suite. The stool is by Reinaldo Sanguino.

Above: Locker room, Caldera House ski club, Jackson Hole, Wyoming, 2016. This custom rug features the downhill racer logo we created for Caldera House. It encapsulates our "Alps meets Tetons" concept. It was inspired by Carlo Mollino, an avid skier, and is meant to evoke the branding irons used by ranchers.

Above: Guest suite, Caldera House ski club, Jackson Hole, Wyoming, 2016.

Right: Kitchen, Steven Johanknecht's apartment, Los Angeles, California, 2018. Honed Carrara marble and red oak line a niche in the corner of the room.

Guest suite, Caldera House ski club, Jackson Hole, Wyoming, 2016. In the Taupo Suite master bath, we put in slate, white oak planks, and nickel Waterworks fixtures.

Reception, Ace Hotel Chicago, Illinois, 2016. Mies van der Rohe and his work in Chicago were central to our concept for this project. We celebrated his love of wood paneling on the walls and ceiling but used stained construction-grade plywood to make it more Ace. The check-in desk is fully covered with black linoleum, and the custom light fixture is by Atelier de Troupe. The bronze wall sculpture, which was cast in ice, is by Steven Haulenbeek.

Left: Dining area, Steven Johanknecht's apartment, Los Angeles, California, 2018. The 1970s Italian leather arm chairs by Matteo Grassi are mixed with a custom walnut table, a George Nelson cabinet, and art collected over many years. The ceramic bowl on the table is by Ettore Sottsass.

Above: Guest room, Ace Hotel Chicago, Illinois, 2016. The ceiling is concrete, and on the built-ins we used construction-grade plywood with a heavy polyurethane varnish, linoleum, and chrome tubing. The wool carpet and blanket by RTH add texture and warmth.

Guest suite kitchens, Caldera House ski club, Jackson Hole, Wyoming, 2016. We designed the interiors of two 6,000-square-foot suites atop the ski club. The two kitchens were created in collaboration with Boffi. The suites have the same layout, but their look and feel are distinctly different.

Left: Master bathroom, Steven Johanknecht's apartment, Los Angeles, California, 2018.

Above: Nickel Dome table lamp for Remains Lighting, 2016.

Carved ceramic canisters by Victoria Morris for Commune, 2015.

Model guest bathroom, Ace Hotel Kyoto, Japan, 2020.

Kitchen, Santa Cruz, California, 2019. This kitchen with soapstone counters is lined with Monterey cypress. On the hood above the stove is plaster by Domingue. The stools are by BDDW, and the pendants are by Areti.

Above: Steven Johanknecht in his apartment, Los Angeles, California, 2018. Next to Steven is a vintage Danish lowboy by George Tanier and a Commune for Christopher Farr rug. The large lithograph is by legendary ceramicist Peter Voulkos.

Right: Bookshelves, Roman Alonso's apartment, Los Angeles, California, 2018. The shelves are solid Douglas fir plank, and they were built by Carl Bronson with invisible supports. They hold a collection of books, ceramics, and personal effects collected for more than thirty years.

Above: Tribal rug by Commune for Christopher Farr, 2017.

Right: Reception, Caldera House ski club, Jackson Hole, Wyoming, 2016. We collaborated with Carney Logan & Burke Architects on this project. The paneling throughout the interior of the building is cedar, except for the walnut-lined seating area in the lobby. The rugs are custom, inspired by Native American motifs, and the furniture is by Michael Boyd.

Above: El Centro Apartments, Hollywood, California, 2018. In the work/lounge sunroom off the pool area we put Nanna Ditzel chairs in bright orange and low tables.

Right: Powder room, Santa Cruz, California, 2019. In this bathroom we used our Circle Drop cement tile for Exquisite Surfaces. The sconces are Branch by Rich Brilliant Willing and the painting is by Theodora Allen.

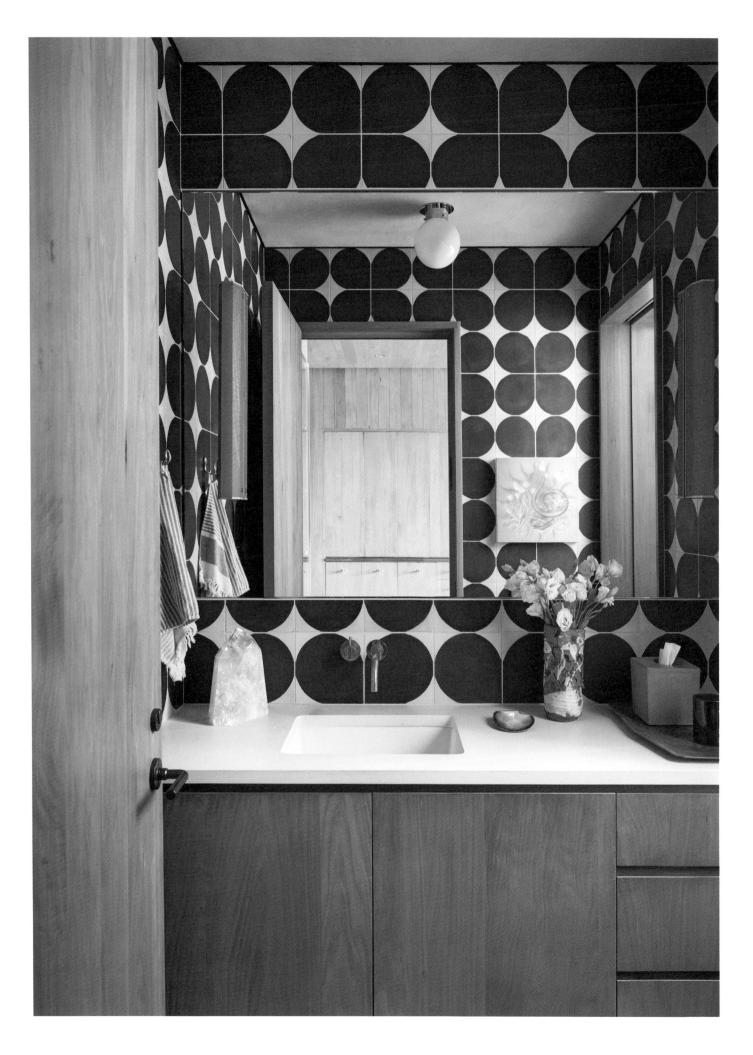

Korek: "Bringing the scents of California flora, burnt Japanese wood, and Viennese leather together never looked so good."

Scenter, Commune by L'Oeil Du Vert, $2,400.

SURFACE 220

221

Left: Bedroom, Roman Alonso's apartment, Los Angeles, California, 2018. The bedside table is by Doug McCollough and was commissioned to work with the plywood bed, a Commune prototype that was never put into production. The bed has a bolster and bedcover made of vintage Japanese fabrics. The bedding is Commune for Hamburg House, and the pillow is by Adam Pogue. The wall sconce is Serge Mouille. The framed photographs on the wall are from Roman's photo collection; these are by Daniel Frasnay, Dennis Hopper, Joseph Sterling, Pirkle Jones, Ron Galella, Osvaldo Salas, Wallace Berman, Joseph Szabo, and Bob Richardson.

Above: L'Oeil du Vert room scenter and fragrance featured in *Surface Magazine*, 2015. Haley Alexander of L'Oeil du Vert created this vaporizing scenter for us, and a custom room fragrance to match. We asked her to take inspiration from the idea of Rudolph Schindler on an imaginary adventure through Japan.

Following: Living room, San Francisco, California, 2019. This room is lined in limewash brick, has elm floors and ceiling, and features a copper fireplace mantel. The custom sofa, by Classic Design, is upholstered in vintage Japanese fabrics hand-quilted by Adam Pogue. The coffee table is by Alma Allen, and the leather lounge chair is by Frits Henningsen. The arm sconce is vintage Belgian by Willy Van Der Meeren, ca. 1953, for Tubax.

PEACE

commune   IMAGE THERAPY · INTERIOR DESIGN · BRAND IDENTITY

Anti-war poster, 2008. This design was inspired by the Weather Underground's famous *Piece Now* poster. The photo is by Bart Cooke.

NOW ²⁰⁰⁸

obertson Blvd. Suite 1 Los Angeles CA 90069 Ph 310 855 9080 www.communedesign.com

Forever Thankful . . .

To Mayer Rus, Matt Tyrnauer, and Lisa Eisner for their insightful words, consistent support, and so much more.

To Michael Sand and Rebecca Kaplan from Abrams for jumping at the chance, and to our editor, Andrea Danese, for making it all happen.

To Stephen Kent Johnson, Leslie Williamson, Spencer Lowell, Mariko Reed, Laure Joliet, Trevor Tondro, Richard Powers, Douglas Friedman, William Waldron, Dominique Vorillon, Adrian Gaut, Matthew Millman, Claudia Lucia, Louis Eisner, and Konstantin Kakanias for making our work look so good.

To our team at Commune, past and present, for their talent and dedication, particularly Dante Iñiguez, for all the hard work on this book.

To our clients for entrusting us with their worlds and for being such wonderful partners.

And finally, to our growing family of artists, artisans, architects, builders, consultants, and craftsmen for their collaborative spirit and soulful work . . . this book is for you.

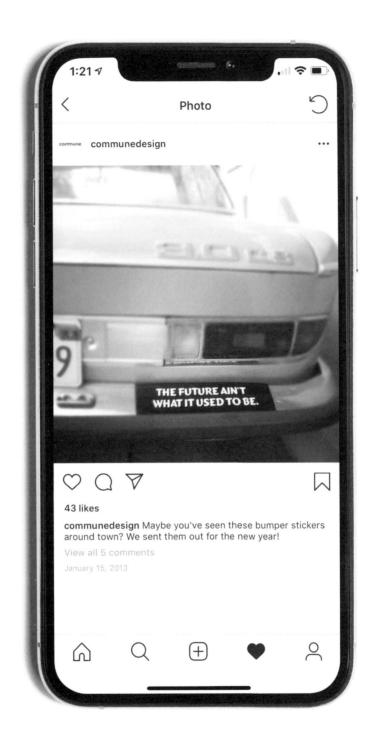

Our first Instagram post, 2013.

Photo Credits

Lisa Eisner: 16

Douglas Friedman: 258, 266, 267

Adrian Gaut: 187, 221, 222–223

Stephen Kent Johnson: 12, 13, 19, 22, 23, 28, 30, 31, 38, 44–45, 47, 48–49,
51, 52, 58, 64, 65, 66, 67, 74–75, 80, 96, 99, 102–103, 109, 126–127, 128,
129, 132–133, 136–137, 138, 144, 147, 148–149, 150, 151, 154, 155, 162–163,
164, 165, 166–167, 168–169, 170, 171, 172–173, 174, 175, 176–177, 184–185,
188–189, 190, 191, 195, 196–197, 199, 200, 201, 203, 204, 205, 212, 213, 214,
215, 216–217, 219, 220, 224–225, 234–235, 236, 237, 247, 248–249, 261, 262,
268, 271, 272–273, 274, 275, 279, 280, 282–283

Laure Joliet: 218, 256, 257

Spencer Lowell: 62, 77, 83, 85, 86-87, 93, 98, 106, 108, 131, 135, 145, 181,
192-193, 198, 207, 208, 209, 229, 230, 231, 232, 233, 238, 239, 242, 243, 246,
254, 255, 256, 259, 263, 277

Claudia Lucia: 32, 40–41, 54–55, 78–79, 95, 100, 101, 104, 107, 111,
112–113, 114-115, 139, 143, 153, 160, 194, 206, 269, 281, 284–285, 287

Matthew Millman: 89, 252–253, 260

Richard Powers: 17, 18, 36–37, 60, 94, 116, 117, 186, 202

Mariko Reed: 92, 182, 240–241

Trevor Tondro: 9, 10–11, 15, 24–25, 26–27, 50, 56–57, 105, 159, 161

Dominique Vorillon: 35, 53, 59, 88, 118, 120–121, 130, 142, 146

William Waldron: 183, 210–211, 278

Leslie Williamson: 20–21, 29, 33, 34, 39, 42, 63, 68–69, 134, 152, 156, 158,
244, 245

Edited by Andrea Danese
Designed by Commune
Production by Alison Gervais

Library of Congress Control Number: 2020931041

ISBN: 978-1-4197-4774-8
eISBN: 978-1-64700-176-6

Text copyright © 2020 Commune Design

Cover © 2020 Abrams

Printed and bound in China
10 9 8 7 6 5 4 3

Abrams books are available at special discounts when purchased in quantity
for premiums and promotions as well as fundraising or educational use.
Special editions can also be created to specification. For details, contact
specialsales@abramsbooks.com or the address below.

Abrams® is a registered trademark of Harry N. Abrams, Inc.

ABRAMS The Art of Books
195 Broadway, New York, NY 10007
abramsbooks.com

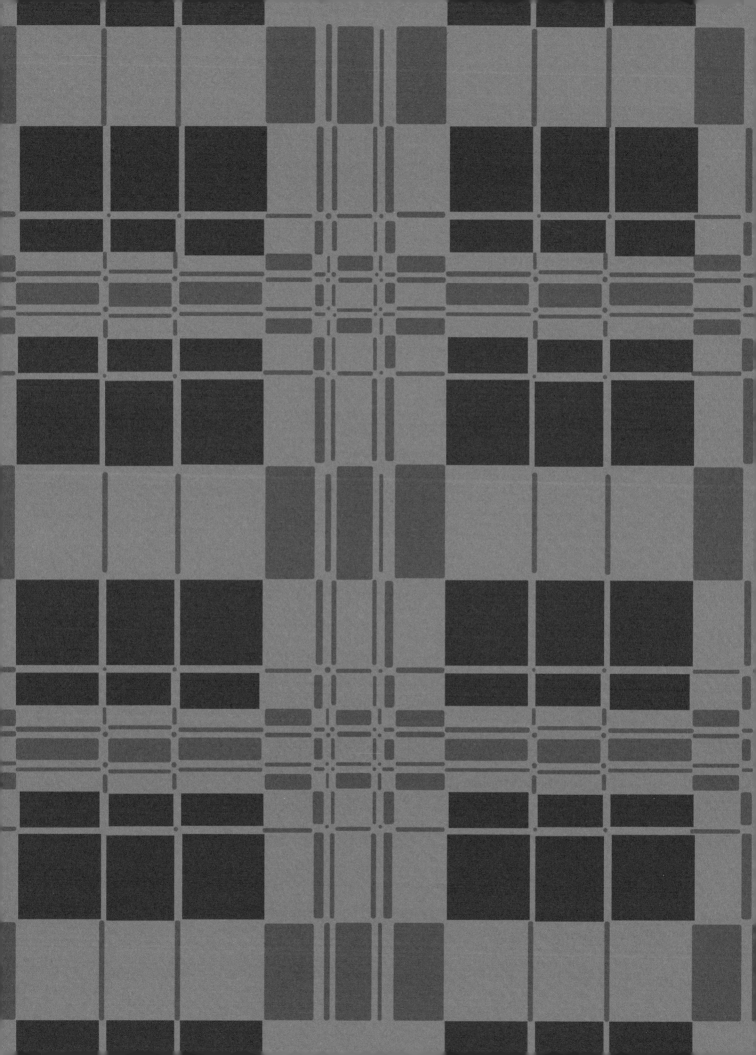